How to Write a Children's Picture Book and Get it Published

Andrea Shavick

A How To Book

ROBINSON

First published in 2011 in Great Britain by How To Books Ltd

This edition published in 2016 by Robinson

Copyright © Andrea Shavick, 2016

1 3 5 7 9 10 8 6 4 2

The moral right of the author has been asserted.

A CIP catalogue record for this book
is available from the British Library.

ISBN: 978-1-47213-579-7 (paperback)
ISBN: 978-1-84803-496-9 (ebook)

Typeset in Garamond by TW Typesetting, Plymouth, Devon
Printed and bound in Great Britain by CPI Group (UK) Ltd, Croydon CR0 4YY

Papers used by Robinson are from well-managed forests and other natural sources

MIX
Paper from
responsible sources
FSC FSC® C104740
www.fsc.org

Robinson
is an imprint of
Little, Brown Book Group
Carmelite House
50 Victoria Embankment
London EC4Y 0DZ

An Hachette UK Company
www.hachette.co.uk

www.littlebrown.co.uk

How To Books are published by Robinson, an imprint of Little, Brown Book Group. We welcome proposals from authors who have first-hand experience of their subjects. Please set out the aims of your book, its target market and its suggested contents in an email to Nikki.Read@howtobooks.co.uk

Contents

Introduction

A PICTURE BOOK WRITER IS BORN

To begin with I want to present to you a very common scenario that occurs at the beginning of the creation of a children's picture book and many a children's writer's career:

1. Parent reads picture book to child.

2. Child enjoys the story and wants said book read another ten million times (or so it feels).

3. Parent, who by now is utterly exhausted and bored silly, suddenly has a brainwave. Hey! This book is so simple, anyone could write stuff like this. Why don't I have a go?

And there you have it. Another would-be picture book writer is born.

It's easy to see why picture books appear to be so easy to write. The plots are simple, the language is basic, the word counts are low and most of the characters are teddy bears. How difficult can it be?

The honest answer is . . . very difficult indeed. Among other things, you need to know what sort of things to write about, what definitely to avoid writing about and how to fit your story into the picture book format, which is something of a skilled job in itself.

Above all you need a reasonable understanding of how the international picture book market works before you have even a glimmer of a chance of getting your book accepted for publication and from there into bookstores around the world and translated into numerous unintelligible but highly impressive-looking foreign languages.

Can you succeed? Well I did. Hundreds, if not thousands, of other children's writers worldwide have succeeded too and so can you. Especially now you have this book, which contains about 15 years' worth of writing and successful publishing experience, insider knowledge and tricks of the trade. Just a quick look at my contents list will demonstrate just how incredibly comprehensive this book is.

So first things first.

WHAT THIS BOOK COVERS

Well obviously it's all about how to write and publish a children's picture book. However, much of the advice is just as applicable to older children's fiction as it is to picture books, especially on the topics of researching publishers, copyright, acceptances, rejections, self-publishing, vanity and online publishing. Other routes to publication via older children's fiction, adult non-fiction and self-publishing are all discussed in the final chapter.

WHAT THIS BOOK DOES NOT COVER

This book does *not* cover the following types of children's books.

ABC and counting books

ABC and counting books are normally written for babies from birth to the age of about 2 years. They usually contain very little text and no story. I'm also including in this category those attractively designed (but mind-numbingly boring) little baby books which have a picture of an everyday object or animal on every page and nothing much else.

Bath books

These are often the same as baby books in content, the only difference being that they're made of plastic so that they can be played with in the bath and then thrown away as soon as they begin to go mouldy (which doesn't bear thinking about!). Bath books have even less content than the baby books described above since the pictures are usually all boats and rubber ducks.

Board books

These are books made entirely of cardboard, as opposed to paper. They are intended to be read to, shared with and handled by babies, and the indestructibleness of the product is specifically engineered to prevent the baby eating it. Which they do, given half a chance! Again, the story content is virtually non-existent.

Novelty books

These are picture books for the very young child from birth to around 3, featuring elaborate devices such as flaps, peep-holes, pop-ups, tabs, sounds and different materials (e.g. fur). In general these books do not contain a lot of story – the product is more like a toy, although there are some notable exceptions.

The reason I do not cover these categories (or genres) of books is because none of them really demand the skill and creativity of an author. And why? Simply because there's no story to write. This means they are, almost without exception, produced in-house by the publisher itself.

By 'in-house' I mean that the entire concept, design and content of the product is created by people who are employed by the publisher. Professional authors are not normally commissioned because there is no creative story-telling work to do.

Your only chance here is if you're an illustrator, since somebody has to design and draw the pictures. More on illustrations later, but for now I will concentrate purely on picture books.

So what is a picture book? Read on . . .

What is a picture book?

1

A 'picture book' is an illustrated story book for very young children from approximately 2 to 5 years old. There will be colour illustrations, usually on every page.

There is text (by 'text' I mean words) but not very much. Most picture books carry just one or two sentences on each page, if that. We are not talking about a full length novel. In fact the total word count will fall somewhere between 100 at the bottom end of the scale to around 600. Of the picture books I've had published, the shortest contained 250 words, the longest had 580.

The text will tell a story but the pictures will also contribute to the 'telling' to a very large extent. The narrative and the pictures work together in a sort of partnership – you can't have one without the other.

A children's picture book is meant to be a shared experience between child and parent (or maybe grandparent, older sibling or teacher). This other person will be physically reading the words and pointing to the pictures. It's important to realise that the child (i.e. the person you are writing for) probably cannot read the actual words.

A picture book story (well the really good ones anyway) will be so interesting and entertaining for the child that they'll want to hear it being read over and over again. This is another important point. After you've finished reading a book that you've chosen for *yourself*, you will normally do one of the following:

◆ Stick it on your bookshelf and forget about it.
◆ Give it to somebody else.

What you will not do is reread it another 50 times. But this is precisely what a young child will expect from a favourite picture book, as all parents know to their cost. This vastly extended 'life expectancy' means that the quality and content of a picture book have to be vastly better and more entertaining than any of its adult counterparts.

In fact I suggest you stop reading this book right now and scoot down to your local library and pick up as many picture books as you can. There is nothing like actually handling and reading a dozen or so to help you understand the product and maybe inspire you as well.

FAMOUS PICTURE BOOKS

Here are some examples of my personal favourites, all of which have been hugely successful:

◆ *The Very Hungry Caterpillar* by Eric Carle.
◆ *The Very Quiet Cricket* also by Eric Carle.

♦ *The Cat in the Hat* by Dr Seuss.
♦ *The Gruffalo* by Julia Donaldson (author) and Axel Scheffler (illustrator)
♦ *Guess How Much I Love You* by Sam McBratney (author) and Anita Geram (illustrator).
♦ *Maisy* by Lucy Cousins.
♦ *Where the Wild Things Are* by Maurice Sendak.
♦ *Mummy Laid an Egg* by Babette Cole.
♦ *Owl Babies* by Martin Waddell (author) and Patrick Benson (illustrator).
♦ *The Queen's Knickers* by Nicholas Allen.
♦ *Six Dinner Sid* by Inga Moore.
♦ *Isabel's Noisy Tummy* by David McKee (and anything else by David McKee).
♦ *I Am Not Sleepy and I Will Not Go to Bed* by Lauren Child.
♦ *Fancy Nancy* by Jane O'Connor (author) and Robin Preiss Glasser (illustrator).

PICTURE BOOK LAYOUT

Now I'm going to describe the actual physical make-up of a picture book. You will find it absolutely invaluable, both from the point of view of familiarising yourself with the product and when it comes to planning and writing your own text.

This template (see Figure 1), various versions of which are used fairly universally by professional children's writers (and similarly described in other 'how-to-write' type books), is based around the 32-page, 12 double-page spread picture book format employed by publishers around the globe.

OTE It may help to have a number of picture
books with you to look at while you read
this section.

Now I will explain some of the technicalities of this particular book format so that you can better understand the physical make-up of the finished product. Note that, although it contains 32 pages, only 24 carry actual story text.

Page 1
This is the front cover, for our purposes counted as page 1.

Pages 2 and 3
These are what are known as 'end papers'. These are pages that appear immediately after you turn over the front cover and open the book. They normally carry no story text but can often include some themed illustration and maybe some sales blurb, such as a list of the author's other titles.

Page 4
This page is often called the 'prelim page'. It's basically the small print and includes information about the publisher, the printer, the date of first publication, ISBN number (International Standard Book Number), copyright notices and possibly even the name of the font used for the text. This is also the most likely location for any dedications from the author and illustrator.

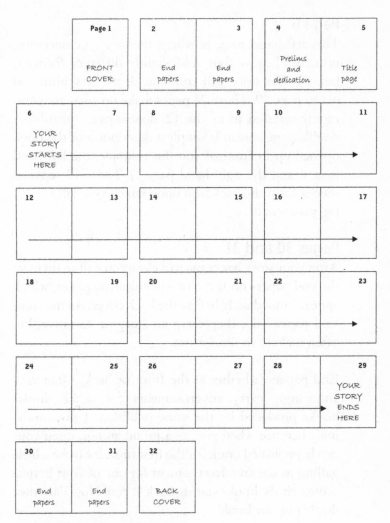

Figure 1. Thirty-two-page picture book layout plan.

Page 5

This right-hand page is usually the 'title page'. This features the name of the book and, unsurprisingly, the title, author and illustrator names, publisher logo and city.

Page 6

This left-hand page is where the story, or narrative, normally begins (but see 'Slightly different formats', below). The story will continue all the way until you get to page 29. These 24 pages make up what are commonly referred to as the 12 'double-page spreads'. A double-page spread is simply a description of the book opened up in front of you (for example, the left-hand page 6 and the right-hand page 7). These 12 separate scenes form the backdrop upon which you will be telling your story.

Pages 30 and 31

After your story has come to a close you will again meet the end papers on these two penultimate pages, which appear immediately before the back cover. As the front 'end papers' do, they carry no story or narrative, but often include an illustration.

End papers (whether at the front or back) often very annoyingly carry advertisements for other similar books produced by the same publisher. I say annoyingly because when you, as a proud author, open your newly published book for the first time, it can be a little galling to see an advertisement for one of your better-selling rivals' books staring back at you. How dare they do that in *your* book!

Page 32

This is the back cover. It will contain a little bit of blurb about the book, maybe a short synopsis of the story or a tiny snippet of text, or perhaps a couple of reviews plus the ISBN, bar code and publisher's details.

SLIGHTLY DIFFERENT FORMATS

If you look at a number of picture books you'll always come across those that do not fit the standard 12 double-page spread layout as described above. The reason for this is that an extra page or two may have been needed either at the beginning or the end of the story. For example, the plot may start fairly slowly, or there might be a bit of scene setting to do which requires extra room, or the story begins on a right-hand page instead of page 6.

Another example would be where the story is extremely visual and the publisher has tried to include as many large illustrations as possible – and has used more than 12 double-page spreads to do this.

Yet another example might be where the story has a twist or surprise ending. In this case it would spoil the surprise to have the ending situated on a right-hand page (i.e. page 29) because the reader would see it the minute they turned over page 27. It's much more effective to take the text right up to page 29 and then place the surprise ending over the page on page 30.

Luckily, as you can see from my layout plan, there are end papers just sitting around doing not very much which allow the publisher to tinker with the layout. By simply bringing the prelims and title page forward to pages 2 and 3, and by running the story right up to page 31, four more pages can be gained *but still allowing the total number of pages to remain at 32.*

Nothing is set in stone – if a publisher falls in love with your text they will work with the illustrator and the art director to sort out the best layout. However, in practice it is *not* a good idea to deviate from the standard format when planning your story.

So do not give your publisher an excuse to reject your work – stick to the 12 double-page spread format as shown on my template layout as closely as you can.

> **NOTE** If you are thinking why 32 pages in total and not, say 38 pages, then the explanation is simple. It's all down to paper folding and international book sizes. There are 24-page picture books produced and also 40-page books – but the vast majority are 32.

So now you have a good idea of what a picture book is, what it physically looks like and how the story text is laid out, it's time to begin thinking about what to write about.

Thinking about your audience

2

WHOM AM I WRITING FOR?

Stop and think for a minute. Do you think you're writing for:

* The child?
* The adult who will read the book to the child?
* The person who will go to the bookshop (or Internet site), choose the book and hand over the money?
* The publisher?

The answer is *all of them!*

First of all the child is your 'target' market. So obviously you have to interest and entertain them.

But equally, because this child will probably be too young actually to read the story for themselves, you also have to interest and entertain the *adult* who will be doing the reading. This could be the parent, grandparent, teacher or even an older sibling and, whoever they are, they'll probably be required to read the book (especially if it's a good one) eight million times, night after night after night.

And again, this long-suffering reader is not necessarily the same person who has actually gone out and bought the book. It could be, but it might just as easily be the child's grandparent, a friend or somebody else entirely. Whoever they are, the purchaser (and, to be honest, this is your favourite person!) will at some point stand and read the book in a bookshop and hopefully be thinking: 'Wow! That is so lovely/sweet/funny/clever/exciting that I'm sure little XYZ will *love* it. Now, where is my credit card?'

Of course the cynical (or maybe the most realistic) answer to the question of whom you are writing for is that none of the above matter so long as you convince the publisher to accept your work.

And if that's not enough, I'm afraid there is a completely different audience you need to write for as well. This is the international audience, made up of children, parents, buyers and publishers around the world.

WHY IS THE INTERNATIONAL AUDIENCE IMPORTANT?

In comparison with publishers of books containing nothing but plain text, picture book publishers have vastly higher costs.

Here are a few reasons why:

♦ As well as the author, an illustrator will also have to be commissioned and paid.

♦ Picture books need to be designed – and designers are expensive.

♦ As well as the illustrator and designer, an art direc-tor will be required to guide and co-ordinate the whole creative production process.

♦ Colour production costs are far higher than black and white.

♦ Higher-quality (and therefore more expensive) paper is needed to ensure the colour illustrations reproduce well.

♦ Higher-quality paper will also be required to prevent the book falling apart in the hands of its intended audience (i.e. small children). Producing a book which is rugged and tough is expensive.

So what is the poor publisher to do if they want to make a profit? Simple. Sell the book around the world. A pic-ture book may not be viable if only marketed in, say, the UK. But sell it into twenty-five other countries and you're talking a whole new ball game in potential sales figures.

Selling a book on the international market is virtually impossible for most publishers to do by themselves because very few of them have a presence in every corner of the globe. So instead what they try to do is sell the *rights* to publish your book in other countries to foreign publishers. These are what are known as rights deals and co-editions.

This means that your picture book story may be accepted and published by, say, Oxford University Press in the UK, but in the USA, China, France, Mexico and so forth, it will be marketed and distributed by completely different publishing houses.

With a number of co-edition deals on board, the unit cost of producing your book will be reduced drastically and your publisher will be able to recoup much of the cost of producing it in their own domain. And why not? All publishers are businesses and all businesses exist to make money. Nobody on the planet will ever publish your book simply because they love it. It's got to have the potential to make money.

This is one of the most important concepts in this book – the fact that, if you want your picture book story to be accepted by a publisher, *you must write for an international audience.*

KEEPING IT INTERNATIONALLY ACCEPTABLE

An internationally acceptable topic (or culturally neutral, if you prefer to use that term) is one that can be understood, recognised and accepted by people all around the world. It's probably easier for me to illustrate this by giving you a few examples of what *not* to write about:

♦ First of all, do not include things in your story which are only used or made or eaten in your particular part of the world. A good example of this is the British Devon cream tea. Australians will not be interested in Devon cream teas or will probably not have even heard of them.

◆ Do not include things in your story which feature prominently in your own local landscape. A good example, also from the UK, is the bright red letter-box. Letterboxes come in different shapes and sizes and colours around the world and some countries don't even have them. Therefore it's impossible to draw a multicultural letterbox. The same applies to the London bus and all other objects of this ilk.

◆ Do not write a story which features specific buildings and places, for example, Buckingham Palace, the Eiffel Tower or Ayers Rock. If you do your publisher will most likely have difficulty selling your story to a publisher in, say, the USA. It's fine to place your action in a non-specific jungle or at the foot of a generic mountain – just don't say which mountain it is!

◆ Also it's best to avoid stories featuring characters wearing local dress or local fashions. Uniforms are another problem area. A postman or a policeman or law-enforcement officer in one country will be dressed completely differently from his or her equivalent elsewhere, so an illustrator would have an impossible task trying to keep this internationally acceptable.

◆ Not just characters and places – be careful when including animal characters too. Try not to use an animal which only features in one particular area of the world and is more or less unknown outside that area. Obviously everybody knows what a tiger is, but not many people around the globe (other than the Brits) would be familiar with, say, hedgehogs.

In other words, if you want to sell your work to a picture book publisher it will have to appeal to everyone, everywhere. Even one little whiff of local colour is enough to deter a publisher.

> **NOTE** Other subjects to avoid are covered in detail in Chapter 5.

The other big problem area when trying to keep your stories internationally acceptable are the characters themselves.

INTERNATIONALLY NEUTRAL CHARACTERS

Generally, writing a picture book depicting characters of any age who are obviously human is disliked by picture book publishers. This is because people from different parts of the world – yes, you guessed it – look different. The illustrator can't draw a 'generic' European-looking child because the publisher may subsequently have difficulty selling the book into the Far East, and vice-versa.

Not only that, but also finding an illustrator who is talented enough to draw realistic-looking children and adults is difficult.

A possible solution to this problem is discussed at the beginning of Chapter 4 – Creating Characters.

NOTE And just in case you are wondering why an editor would not simply contact you and say, 'We love your story but please can you rewrite it without the man in the kilt munching haggis in front of Edinburgh Castle', forget it. They won't bother. Your work will just be rejected.

I will continue to stress this vitally important theme of keeping things internationally acceptable throughout the entire book.

3 *What to write about*

WHAT DO PICTURE BOOK PUBLISHERS WANT?

As every picture book publisher will tell you, a great picture book:

◆ has an 'edge';
◆ is exciting, or maybe so sweet you want to hug it;
◆ has a very strong plot that can stand being read over and over;
◆ isn't too complicated – so no flashbacks, wrinkles in time, complicated subplots, etc.;
◆ is linear (i.e. has a beginning, a middle and an ending all in that order). No beginning with the punch-line and then saying 'Two days earlier'. You're not writing a soap opera;
◆ is completely different from all the books that came before . . . but not so different they won't be able to sell it;
◆ has a twist or otherwise unexpected ending that makes you go 'ahhhh' (more on endings below);
◆ includes a location, a plot and characters which are all internationally acceptable;

- includes at least one character who is appealing and memorable enough to be utilised again in a follow-up book or series of books;
- has merchandising potential (i.e. characters who can be turned into toys); and
- last but no means least, contains a blissfully happy ending. And if it can't be blissfully happy, then at least fairly uplifting or sweet. Picture books never end in tears!

This may seem a tad cynical but, actually, I'm being completely honest. This is what picture book publishers all over the world are looking for – enormous sales potential!

THE SEVEN STORY PLOTS

You will probably be familiar with the theory that there are only seven story plots in the entire world and that virtually every tale that's ever been written fits into one of these categories. In fact there are a number of books which support this viewpoint, probably the most famous being *The Seven Basic Plots: Why We Tell Stories* by Christopher Booker. Although not all seven archetypal plots are suitable for use in a picture book, I will list them briefly here.

Overcoming the monster

In this plot the protagonist (your hero or main character) finds themselves faced with an enormous challenge usually involving (or personified by) a monster. The hero's challenge is to defeat the monster and save the day.

The Gruffalo by Julia Donaldson and Axel Scheffler is a good example of this as it features a fearsome monster reputed to have 'Terrible teeth in his terrible jaws.' Other examples from children's literature would be *Little Red Riding Hood*, *The Three Little Pigs* and, for adults, *James Bond* fits the bill nicely.

Rags to riches

Cinderella and *The Ugly Duckling* are good examples of the rags-to-riches plotline. At the beginning of the story an ordinary, nothing-special sort of character is shown being ignored or treated badly or simply suffering from a lack of self-esteem. By the end of the story they've found the means to transform themselves and subsequently live happily ever after.

My own picture book, *You'll Soon Grow, Alex*, is another example of this – basically it's about a little boy with low self-esteem who discovers happiness.

> **NOTE** A rags-to-riches plotline normally has nothing to do with money (e.g. winning the lottery, etc.).

The quest

Your main character is obliged (often unwillingly) to go on a long, tortuous, demanding journey in order to save somebody or something, or even the entire world.

From teenage literature, *His Dark Materials*, *Lord of the Rings* and *Harry Potter* are good examples of this, and a gentler example from the world of picture books is *How to Catch a Star* by Oliver Jeffers.

Voyage and return

Often interchangeable with the plot just described, voyage and return usually involves the main character travelling into a different or unfamiliar world. After an initial excitement and sense of wonderment, it soon becomes apparent that danger lurks around every corner and, ultimately, escape becomes imperative.

The best-selling picture book, *We're Going on a Bear Hunt*, is a good example of this and, for older children, *Alice in Wonderland* and *His Dark Materials*.

Comedy

The stuff of romantic fiction, comedy often involves an intricate plot full of misunderstandings which are resolved in the end with the hero or heroine living happily ever after.

The wonderful books of Jane Austen are a good example of this but, for obvious reasons, romance isn't normally a feature of picture books as the audience is far too young for such things. However, there are plenty of picture books about friendship, of which Oliver Jeffers' *Lost and Found* is but one and *The Bad-tempered Ladybird* by Eric Carle is another. In fact many picture books have a gentle humour.

Tragedy

Pure tragedy by definition involves a main character, usually high born or holding down a prominent position in society, who though some inherent flaw in their character is drawn towards ruin, disaster and death.

Again, not really a recipe for a picture book since publishers of young children's books normally expect a happy ending, but there are still some notable exceptions, such as the wonderful *Not Now, Bernard* by David McKee in which a little boy whose parents ignore him is eaten by a monster. Good examples from adult literature include *Othello*, *Macbeth*, *Romeo and Juliet* and *Oedipus*.

Rebirth

Here the hero/heroine finds themselves manoeuvred into a position where they are controlled by a villain or other deadly force. Liberation is usually forthcoming with the appearance of an archetypal knight on a white horse or through the power of love and sacrifice. Think *Snow White*.

Rebirth could also be seen as the dawning of understanding or the beginning of friendship where previously there was animosity and hatred. Take a look at David McKee's *Two Monsters* and you'll see what I mean.

Many stories contain elements of more than one plot. For example, *Cinderella* is both a rags-to-riches and a rebirth plot and *The Gruffalo* is, to my mind, a mix of voyage/return and overcoming the monster (with an unexpected twist in which, instead of destroying the monster, the protagonists run away from it!). Other picture books endow a well-known plotline with an unexpected and usually humorous twist.

I suggest you borrow lots of picture books from your local library and see if you can identify which of the seven plots has been employed by their authors. It's an interesting exercise and one that will help you understand the creative process as well as giving you lots of ideas to work with.

WRITING BOOKS ABOUT ISSUES

There is a lot of advice out there that says, if you are a picture book writer, you must not cover an issue because it will look like an educational book or, even worse, a book that will languish in the parent section of the library and bookshop and never make it on to the front shelves as a stand-alone picture book.

By 'issue' I am really talking about such titles as *Jenni goes to the Dentist, Hannah has a Hair Cut* or *Shiv is Scared of the Dark*. Important though they are, these books are primarily written to familiarise young children with commonplace events and also to assist them in making sense of difficult situations.

These sorts of books are usually short (24 pages) and explain in straightforward, matter-of-fact language the event described by the title, and as such are not really picture book writing territory.

This is chiefly because it doesn't take a vast skill to write:

Jeremy visited the dentist.

The dentist looked at his teeth.

Afterwards the dentist gave Jeremy a sticker for being such a good boy.

Do you see what I mean? It's so straightforward most junior editors could rustle up the text standing on their heads. The skill of a picture book author in creating wonderful plots and characters alongside an engaging story-telling manner is not required. For this reason, simple issue books are normally written 'in-house' by the publishing staff themselves so you, the creative writer, will not get a look in.

Having said that, many authors use an issue or a problem as the basis for their picture book work. My picture book, *The Truth About Babies*, concerned a little girl who has a new baby brother and consequently feels very left out. Typical issue material – older sibling who's jealous of the new baby.

Although my book is often found in the parents section of children's libraries it is not an instruction manual for how to deal with jealousy. On the contrary, the story deals with the main character's journey through initial annoyance and upset towards the building of a stronger bond with her mother and a real affection for her younger sibling.

This is the difference between a pure issue book and a picture book. The picture book uses the issue as the basis for an imaginative story in which the feelings of the main characters are explored alongside an innovative solution to the initial problem.

Some other good examples are as follows:

♦ *I Will Not Ever Never Eat a Tomato* by Lauren Child, which is about a child who hates vegetables.
♦ *Owl Babies* by Martin Waddell, in which separation issues are explored within a story about three baby owls whose mother has flown away and may never return.
♦ *Where the Wild Things Are* by Maurice Sendak, in which a little boy is angry and unhappy after having been told off by his mother.
♦ *Tusk Tusk* by David McKee, in which the very adult issue of racism and intolerance is explored in a story about two elephant races (a white one and a black one) who attempt to annihilate each other.

So by all means cover an 'issue'. Just remember you are aiming for a fresh, original and readable take on the subject, not an instruction manual.

USING FAIRY TALES, MYTHS AND LEGENDS

Picture books which deal with fairy tales, myths and legends go in and out of fashion on a regular basis (and when I say fashion I mean the enthusiasm by which they are greeted by commissioning editors).

Of course, I am only talking about *reworkings* of stories in which an author tells a well-known story but comes at it from a completely new angle or viewpoint.

I am not talking about an existing story in which the author has simply written out, say, *Goldilocks and the*

Three Bears in their own words. No publisher would ever be interested in that because the characters and plot wouldn't possess a single scrap of originality.

Using Goldilocks as our example, a reworking of the subject matter might result in the story being told from Baby Bear's point of view with Goldilocks as a baddie. After all, she does enter his home without permission, eat his food, break his furniture and sleep in his bed.

Here are some examples of successful picture books in which the author has used characters (or other elements) of well-known fairy tales or legends and to create a brand-new, fresh story:

♦ *Mixed up Fairytales* by Hillary Robinson and Nick Sharratt.
♦ *Big Bad Wolf is Good* by Simon Puttock.
♦ *The Pea and the Princess* by Mini Grey (told from the pea's point of view!).
♦ *Snow White and the Seven Aliens* by Laurence Anholt.
♦ *The Truth about Hansel and Gretel* by Karina Law.

To sum up – the use of famous fairy tales, myths and legends as inspiration for new and unique stories is perfectly acceptable. Plain copying is not.

NOTE You do find famous fairy tales and legends being rewritten (as opposed to being reworked) by experienced and very well established writers, but normally this is done to showcase an illustrator's work so that people all over the world can buy the book primarily for the beautiful pictures.

BRAINSTORMING FOR IDEAS

There are literally thousands of topics you can write about. Just get yourself a very large notebook or exercise book and start to list some of the things in a child's life that you think they may want to read about. What you're aiming for is to find something *you* will feel inspired to write about.

Here are some examples of themes/topics to start you off, with one or two particularly good picture book examples:

Stories built around children's daily lives
- Getting up.
- Bedtime – see *I Don't Want To Go To Bed* by Tony Ross.
- Bath time.
- Meal times – see *I Will Not Ever Never Eat a Tomato* by Lauren Child.
- Getting dressed.
- Potty training or other bodily functions – see *I Want My Potty* by Tony Ross.

◆ Household visitors – see *The Tiger Who Came to Tea* by Judith Kerr.

Stories in which characters go somewhere

◆ To nursery school.
◆ Out shopping.
◆ To visit somebody.
◆ On holiday.
◆ On a journey by train, bus, plane, car, bike, walking, etc.
◆ On an adventure – see *We're Going on a Bear Hunt* by Michael Rosen.
◆ To the beach.

Stories about possessions

Teddy bears and toys (and especially their loss) – see *Elmer and the Lost Teddy* by David McKee and *Where Are You Blue Kangaroo?* by Emma Chichester Clark.

Stories about feelings

◆ Jealousy – often of younger or older sibling.
◆ Being frightened – e.g. the monster under the bed theme.
◆ Love – see *Guess How Much I Love You* by Sam McBratney.
◆ Anger – see *Where the Wild Things Are* by Maurice Sendak.
◆ Embarrassment – see *Isabel's Noisy Tummy* by David McKee.
◆ Excitement about a forthcoming event.
◆ Sharing – see *The Bad-tempered Ladybird* by Eric Carle.
◆ Worries.
◆ Lack of self-esteem.

◆ Guilt, maybe about doing something 'naughty' – see *Oscar Got the Blame* by Tony Ross.
◆ Sadness – such as coming to terms with the death of a pet or a beloved grandparent.

Stories about family situations

◆ Sibling rivalry.
◆ Busy parents – see *Not Now Bernard* by David McKee.
◆ New baby.
◆ Getting to know step-brothers and sisters.
◆ Family parties and get-togethers.
◆ Noisy families – see *Peace At Last* by Jill Murphy.
◆ Parents who are always late.
◆ Parents or other family members who are embarrassing.

There are so many categories, I could fill an entire book with them. Furthermore, every single idea opens out into thousands of individual possibilities. If I just take the theme of sibling rivalry, literally hundreds if not thousands of books have been written on the subject and all are utterly different.

For example, you could write about the following:

◆ Jealousy of an older/younger sibling.
◆ Rivalry or other clash between siblings.
◆ A sibling who is very annoying/funny/silly.
◆ A sibling who does naughty things for which the other one gets the blame.
◆ A sibling who copies the other one.
◆ A sibling who turns out to be a monster in disguise!

Goodness, I could carry on indefinitely. In fact, why not take your exercise book and see whether you can think up another ten ideas for the sibling theme.

If you don't particularly want to write about something based around a child's life and experience then there are plenty of other themes to explore. For example:

♦ The lifecycle of an animal – see *The Very Hungry Caterpillar* by Eric Carle. Obviously you have the entire animal kingdom from which to choose.
♦ Imaginary creatures or alien monsters – see *I'm Coming To Get You* by Tony Ross.
♦ Pet adventures – see *Six Dinner Sid* by Inga Moore.

Take your exercise book and start compiling your own list and keep going and going until the muse strikes you. But don't be discouraged if inspiration doesn't materialise immediately. Good brainstorming is a little bit like turning on a furred-up, rusty tap – at first you need a huge effort to produce even a few drops of water but once you get going it should start gushing out.

Using memory

One way to narrow down the options, and also to make your stories highly original, is to use material that is utterly and completely unique to you. Yes, I'm talking about your memory. An author's memory is always their very best resource, especially when it comes to children's books. The reason is simple. Everyone has experienced childhood.

You can either use memories of your own childhood or memories of things that happened when your own children or grandchildren (if you have them) were young.

So get out your notebook or exercise book again, take yourself off somewhere comfortable when you won't be disturbed, close your eyes and journey back in time.

Write down whatever pops into your head. Don't worry about whether the material is usable or not. Don't think about whether it's silly or even plain ridiculous. Simply concentrate on reliving your past and getting something down on paper. Here are some ideas to start you off in your journey back in time:

- Where did you live as a small child? What was the place like? A house? A flat? A houseboat? A caravan? A palace? What did it look like? What did it feel like? What did it smell like?
- Was your family home noisy, crowded, busy, empty, silent? What did your home sound like? How did you feel about that? Do you wish it could have been different?
- What was your bedroom like? Did you share it with somebody else and, if so, how did you feel about that? How did you get along? What did you argue about? How did you create your own personal space?
- What were your worries and fears? Were you scared of anything? Did anyone help you conquer your fears and, if so, how?
- Did you have any longstanding family traditions? For example, did you always go to the same place on holiday, have a huge BBQ every summer or the same sing-song round the piano at Christmas?

- How did you or your siblings react to new experiences? For example, the first time at the beach, first day at school, first swimming lesson, first time you got lost, came face to face with the neighbour's dog, had a haircut, climbed a tree, went on a boat, etc.
- Did you and your family have any particular sayings or in-jokes that could be used as the basis for a story?
- Are there any particular events that stand out in your memory? Did you ever get into terrible trouble? Did anything particularly disastrous happen?
- Think about the stories you've told your friends about your childhood – the things you particularly remember. For example, what happened the first time you went to the seaside? What did you do? What did your siblings do or say? What you're looking for here are humorous things, things that always made your family laugh.
- Did you ever go out exploring? Where did you go? What did you do? What sort of adventures did you have?
- Did you move home frequently? If so, then why? How did that affect you?
- Is there anything about your childhood you particularly enjoyed, or hated, or wished you could have changed?

Memory exercises are incredibly effective at dredging up happenings in your past that you've completely forgotten about. Apart from providing wonderful story material, journeying back in time may leave you with a huge sense of satisfaction, or happiness, or sadness, or wistfulness, or maybe even a previously unrealised insight into the feelings, motivation and behaviours of members of your family.

In the next chapter we will continue to explore how memory can be utilised to create believable and unique characters.

ENDINGS

Endings for picture books really have to be happy, or at least uplifting. Of course there are always exceptions to this rule, but in general, little children need gentleness and reassurance, not tears before bedtime. Some of the larger world markets (for example, the USA) seem to have a definite preference for happy endings. So if you want your book to sell in bucket-loads, always ensure your protagonists succeed in their quests, solve their problems and escape from the monster. OK, it's not reality but then, for the most part, picture books are not realistic.

It's also better to have a definite, easily understood ending; ambiguous endings which are open to inter-pretation are unlikely to succeed. If the Big Bad Wolf jumped down the chimney but then we never found out whether he ate the three little pigs or received his comeuppance it would have been most unsatisfying. Your young audience would be for ever asking their parents 'What happened next?'

Once you have the bare bones of the story you can progress to a spot of plot-planning as described in Chapter 7.

4 *Creating characters*

Before we begin fleshing out characters, it's important to think about some of the more basic ideas, such as whether your protagonists are human or not, how old they are, whether they are male or female and what their names are. Note that these decisions all relate to the theme I keep coming back to – international acceptability (and therefore saleability).

HUMAN OR ANIMAL? WHAT DO PUBLISHERS PREFER?

I have already discussed why it is vitally important to make every aspect of your picture book internationally acceptable and, of course, this includes your characters. What you must do is avoid characters who are too localised.

If you include characters who are immediately identifiable to a specific part of the world or local culture, race or religion, then you risk alienating potential foreign publishers and having your work summarily rejected, even if your basic plot and text are good.

But how can you create culturally neutral characters when people around the world *do* look physically different? The simple answer is – don't use human characters. Use *animal* characters instead.

Actually there is another very practical reason why picture book publishers tend to shy away from texts describing human characters. It's because surprisingly few illustrators are capable of drawing them! For some reason it's much easier to draw a cute, cuddly tiger than a human child.

Why do you think there are so many picture books featuring cute little rabbits, bears, lions, tigers, elephants, ducks, teddies and toys? It's a no-brainer. Not only are they easier to draw, wherever you go in the entire world a bear is a bear is a bear! Illustrators can draw them, everybody will recognise them and the problem of how to keep characters internationally acceptable so that the book can be sold around the world is solved.

Having said that, there are certain illustrators who are very adept at creating 'cartoon'-type characters. By this I mean characters who are obviously human but defy all attempts to categorise them into a specific ethnic group. The characters created by the illustrators Lauren Child, Korky Paul and Russell Ayto are good examples of this, so it can be done. But if you want to give yourself a fighting chance of having your work accepted for publication I would say stick to animal characters.

CREATING NON-HUMAN CHARACTERS

So what does this mean when it comes to writing your text? How do you indicate to a potential publisher that your character is an animal and not a human being?

Not that much really. First of all you need to avoid obvious references to humans and the things only humans can do:

- ◆ Lucy scratched her turned-up, freckled nose.
- ◆ Luke pulled up his socks.
- ◆ Sophie wiggled her fingers and did a handstand.

OK, there might be a few animals who could manage these behaviours but, in general, these examples are purely human. So avoid them. This will entail reading your text very carefully to see how the words could be interpreted.

Another thing you can do is to consider changing the names of your characters so that they are more obviously un-human. Big Bear and Little Bear (well not *that* exactly, because it's been done before) are probably a safer bet than, say, Sophie and Rachel. More on names shortly.

If you *must* write about human children maybe consider upping your age group and writing for 7–11-year-olds. Many books for this age group are marketed, at least initially, in their home markets alone (i.e. just in the UK or just in the USA) and therefore there isn't so much emphasis on keeping things international. And books for teenagers do not usually include pictures anyway, or very few, so the problem rarely arises.

Having said this, picture book publishers *do* accept books written ostensibly about real children in real-life situations, and several of my own picture books are living proof of this. But I did find, in each case, that the publisher spent a very long time mulling over whether or not (and how) to turn my characters into animals.

> **NOTE** It's probably best to avoid pigs and other animals which may cause offence to certain religions. De-pig your farmyard!

ALIENS

Alien characters are another way of sidestepping the problem of how to keep a story culturally and internationally acceptable. Interestingly, you don't see many picture books featuring aliens and I'm not sure why. Maybe it's because publishers feel the 'other world' concept is simply too difficult for a young child to grasp.

To a young child a book about a teddy or a couple of bunny rabbits would instantly make sense. A book about an alien . . . well it's not something that they would have come across very often.

DEVELOPING CHARACTERS WITH SERIES POTENTIAL

One type of character publishers are always on the lookout for are those who are so strong, so interesting and so unusual that they can be employed over and over, not only in follow-up books but also marketed in the form of soft toys.

A brilliant example of a character who lends itself perfectly to international brand merchandising is Elmer, the star of *Elmer the Patchwork Elephant* created by the British author, David McKee. There are over 20 books featuring Elmer, millions of children now own an Elmer teddy and there's even a children's TV series.

Wikipedia describes Elmer as 'an elephant with a colourful body, with yellow, orange, red, pink, purple, blue, green, black and white arranged as a patchwork'.

Not only is Elmer internationally acceptable (or culturally neutral, if you prefer that term), visually he is hugely interesting and his easily recognisable coloured patchwork is an art director's dream.

But there is another facet of Elmer that makes him even more interesting (apart from his physical appearance), and that is his quirky personality. Not only is Elmer cheerful and good-natured but he also loves playing practical jokes on his friends.

So how is it possible to create a realistic 'personality' for a baby lion or a teddy bear or a rabbit? One tried and tested successful method is to base them on a real person.

BRAINSTORMING FOR CHARACTERS

As discussed in the previous chapter, your own memory is always going to be a fertile source of inspiration when creating characters with realistic personalities.

And once again, take yourself (and your notebooks) to a quiet place with minimal disturbance, close your eyes and travel back in time to your own childhood to discover your very own unique inspiration:

♦ Think about your brothers or sisters or step-brothers and sisters and their friends. What were they like? What were their worries and fears? What made them fun? How did they make you laugh? What made each of them different or memorable?

♦ Now think about other people you knew as a small child, such as neighbours, teachers, friends and parents of friends. What were they like? How would you describe their personalities, their body language, the gestures they made? If you liked them, try to analyse why. Look out for any quirky or silly or endearing behaviour that stands out in your memory.

♦ Now think about your parents. Did they exhibit any annoying or funny mannerisms or behaviours? Were you proud of them? Were you embarrassed by them?

♦ Did any of your family, friends and neighbours have any particular 'catch-phrases' or in-jokes which you remember?

♦ Also, don't neglect your own childhood imaginings. Did you have any favourite possessions, or toys or teddies? What were their names, and why? What characteristics and personality traits did you endow them with? What adventures did they have?

Hopefully you will find this exercise a source of inspiration, but your work isn't finished yet.

Once you have a number of possible ideas, I suggest you get to know these potential characters a little better. Authors of teenage and adult fiction create character 'profiles', so why shouldn't you?

For each character in your story, even the peripheral ones, you need to know the following:

♦ How old is this character?
♦ What do they look like?
♦ What clothes, if any, do they wear?
♦ What do they like doing?
♦ Do they have any friends and, if so, who?
♦ How do they enjoy themselves?
♦ Where do they live?
♦ Whom do they live with?
♦ Are they confident or shy, extroverted or introverted?
♦ How do they see themselves? Do they like themselves? If not, why not?
♦ Are they grumpy, or happy, or curious, or hungry, or scared, or angry, or dissatisfied, or lonely, or naughty?
♦ How do they normally spend their day?
♦ How would they *like* to spend their day?

- ◆ Do they have any problems or worries?
- ◆ Are they scared of anything?
- ◆ What do they want out of life?

Obviously this is not an exhaustive list. But you can see what I'm saying. By creating a character profile, by taking the time to think about and write down all that character's likes and dislikes, physical characteristics and personality traits you will really be on the road to making them come alive.

Once you begin writing your story, keep your list close at hand and refer to it on a regular basis.

> **NOTE** Remember to ensure all your characters have different characters, personality traits and appearances. This helps readers understand your story better and not get muddled up.

Listing your characters' attributes is also useful in helping your story remain consistent throughout (see the discussion on consistency in Chapter 10).

CHARACTER AGES

Whether human or animal, most picture book characters are young.

If human, show your characters as slightly older than your intended audience. For example, if your story is intended for 3-year-olds, make your characters do and say things which a 4–5-year-old might aspire to do.

Whatever you do, avoid main characters who are much younger than your target audience. Children do not want to read stories where the main characters do things which they would consider babyish. For example, a 4-year-old would not identify with a main character who wears a nappy or drinks bottle milk. Let your readers aspire to be a little older than they are.

If, on the other hand, children *do* like reading about baby animals, the age and actions of animal characters are not so important. Of course, I am talking about your main characters here. They should always be young simply so that your reader can identify with them.

Peripheral characters can of course be older or younger, or completely grown-up. It's perfectly acceptable for your main character to interact in your story with an older or younger sibling, a parent, a grandparent, a teacher or even a 300-year-old alien!

Should your main character be male or female?

I don't think it really matters what sex your main character is. It has been said boys prefer male heroes, but you also hear industry 'experts' recommending the use of female characters.

In my experience, if a publisher loves your story but particularly wants a book with a male/female protagonist, they will simply change the sex of your main character to suit themselves. If your story is a good one, gender will not matter.

Of course if you name your main character Percy Pig then you are signalling to the publisher that he is clearly a boy. Writing about Baby Bear is more vague and therefore probably a better bet – although personally I think Baby Bear sounds like a boy.

Older characters, such as adults in your story, can be either sex (although see the discussion on sexism in the next chapter). In any case, it will be the illustrator's job to visualise the characters and bring them to life. Your job is to concentrate on the story.

ALIVE OR INANIMATE?

Although *Thomas the Tank Engine* is wildly successful, it is difficult to endow an inanimate object (like a car or a tree or a plane) with the dreams and aspirations and interesting personality traits required of a picture book character. Therefore I'd recommend sticking to 'live' characters (i.e. human, animal or alien) and ditching that Rosy the Rosebush idea as quickly as possible.

CHARACTER NUMBERS

How many characters should you have in your picture book story? I'd say one or two main characters, or maybe three *at the very most*. If absolutely necessary to the story you can also include various peripheral characters but really no more than three. Keep it simple.

NAMING YOUR CHARACTERS

I touched on gender issues when naming characters above, but finding good names is difficult. If you want to pick 'real' names then it's important to keep them as international as possible.

Try to resist using your own children's names. Unless they are universally popular names around the world, you'll just appear amateurish.

To check on the usability and international status of different names you can easily go online and search. Just type in 'most popular names around the world' or 'most popular baby names' and you'll soon find yourself scrolling through hundreds of fascinating websites.

At the time of writing I did just that and discovered that, for example, the name Sophie (and variants of it) is wildly popular around the globe. I'm not recommending you name your protagonist Sophie or Sophia, but it's useful to be aware of this ready source of information. Bookshops invariably carry books of names (usually in the baby section).

Don't overlook the possibility of endowing your characters with names which are usually used as surnames or family names. Once you veer off the beaten track and start considering place names, object names, plant names and so on (Peanut Butter, Marmite, Paddington, Willow, Elmer, Maisy – to name some famous examples), there are literally millions of possibilities to choose from.

You may decide not to use any 'proper' names at all. Did you notice how many of the bestselling picture books I listed at the beginning of this book do not use proper names for their main characters? *The Very Hungry Caterpillar* and *The Very Quiet Cricket* and *The Cat in the Hat* and *Mummy Laid an Egg* feature strong characters but none of them has a particular name. Even *The Gruffalo* doesn't have a name (he is *a* gruffalo – he isn't actually named Gruffalo).

Often character names can be descriptive. *Guess How Much I Love You* by Sam McBratney and Anita Geram features a character called Nutbrown Hare, and he is, you guessed it, a nutbrown hare. Many other successful picture books feature characters with descriptive names. Maybe yours can do so too.

Once you have a shortlist of names, go online again and check them out using a search engine and one or two large book retailers, such as Amazon. This is a good way to find out whether your name, or book title, has been used before. If it has then you'll have to go back to the drawing board.

In the end it's best to concentrate on writing your story, as you might spend years choosing the most marvellously unique character names only to find your editor (or an editor working for one of your overseas publishers) changes all of them.

5 Subjects to avoid

I'm afraid that if you're writing picture books, you have to be very, very careful with your subject matter. Whatever they say to the contrary, publishers all over the world are utterly obsessed about making sure their books don't offend anyone.

For example, a few years ago I had a book title which included the word banana. Yes that's right – the fruit. But because the publisher was worried the word 'banana' might upset people (they said it could be used as a derogatory term) my title was scrapped and we ended up with something completely different and nowhere near as good.

Now although this was not a picture book the basic premise is the same. If you want your picture book published, you have to tread carefully when it comes to subject matter.

I have already explained why anything connected with your particular locality or country is best avoided in order to keep your book as internationally acceptable as possible, but unfortunately there are plenty of other things to avoid as well. I will now explore some of them in a little more detail.

SEXISM

Avoid this like the plague. Keep away from showing professional people, such as doctors and dentists, as always being male and try to avoid having female characters/mummy bunny rabbits, etc., undertaking stereotypical 'woman's work', such as washing, cooking, ironing, shopping, mending clothes or helping children with homework. I've probably omitted 95 other things, but you get the picture.

Why not? Well it's not PC, and anyway women don't do stuff like that anymore (did I mention that the entire publishing industry lives in cloud-cuckoo land?).

The PC-ness of picture books seems to have stifled a lot of creativity and reality for the sake of – well I'm not sure what it's for – but that's the book business for you.

There is only one exception and that's where you include a character whom your young reader will 'recognise' as playing a stereotypical role in their own life. So for now, at least, a mummy should be female, a daddy should be male and a nursery teacher is virtually always female because, let's face it, most nursery teachers *are* female so keep them that way.

CLASSISM

Don't write about happy, two-parent, middle-class families living in nice houses as apparently they don't exist any longer (and you might upset all those who don't fit neatly into that category).

So no stories that call for pictures of nice houses with gardens or anything else that necessitates the characters looking like they might have a bit of money stashed away . . . like a swimming pool or children being taken in big cars to fancy schools. Or people enjoying an expensive holiday, especially on a cruise ship.

To spell this out, no text with anything like 'Lucy ran into the garden and jumped into the swimming pool'.

It's perfectly acceptable to have animals jumping into a waterhole in some faraway jungle as I did in my picture book, *Stop, Elephant, Stop!*, but you should avoid describing characters jumping into a private swimming pool in an affluent neighbourhood *or anything else that spells money.*

RACISM

Racism is totally unacceptable anyway, let alone in a children's book. If the whole point of your book is to show how bad racism is, it's still a difficult concept for a young child to grasp so is best avoided.

RELIGION

Religion is another topic that doesn't marry well with picture book fiction. For a start, religious beliefs vary widely throughout the world and, by giving your story a religious feel or theme, you could alienate overseas publishers.

Another reason to avoid religion, anti-religion and even the topics listed below under 'witches' is because little kids won't understand it – ideas about belief systems are simply too complex for very young children to grasp.

It could be argued that, in the USA, there is a large and potentially growing 'religious' market but, unless you are specifically targeting that sector, by including religious characters, bible stories, religious beliefs or rituals or even religious festivals such as Christmas in your story, you will be automatically excluding everybody else in the world and thereby restricting your potential sales market.

And any perceived restriction to worldwide sales will be the kiss of death to your chances of having the story accepted.

WITCHES

Yes, I know that *Harry Potter* is a rather large exception to this rule but for picture books it really is best to avoid witches. Even though there are a number of successful 'witch' picture books (for example, *Winnie the Witch* by Valarie Thomas and Korky Paul, whose illustrations are just wonderful), to play it safe and give yourself the best chance of being published the whole concept of witches and witchcraft should really be avoided.

This may sound draconian but if you insist on covering this topic there are large sections of the world who will simply not buy your book. Witches, wizards, pagan rituals, religious rituals, magic, people praying, religious festivals are all out, I'm afraid, if you want to give yourself the best possible chance of being published.

DANGEROUS SITUATIONS

Another area to avoid is showing or describing any sort of dangerous situation which a child could potentially copy – so never have your main character jumping out of a window and flying away (sorry, Peter Pan, you've been rejected!).

Other 'danger' items include fireworks, balloons, candles – which are banned in some countries – guns, weapons, kids playing near roads, rivers, streams, roads full of traffic and so on.

Even the harmless torch shouldn't be included since in some countries the word torch means incendiary device.

SCARY STUFF, HORROR AND VAMPIRES

Don't write anything scary unless your age group is over 10, which for a picture book it isn't. Nobody will buy a picture book for a 3-year-old which will prevent them going to sleep. The idea is to be all cuddly and lovely and now it's time for lights out, see you in the morning. You don't want to scare them to death!

With this in mind, none of your stories should describe a character being injured, hurt, abused, scared, chased by ghosts or vampires, or dead people . . . or, to be perfectly honest, even crying.

My protagonist in *You'll Soon Grow, Alex* is actually quite miffed because he's short. Although I describe him as being very unhappy, he still doesn't actually cry. In fact he appears to be positively chirpy and cheerful all the way through.

There *are* books about being scared of things like monsters under the bed, and being scared of the dark, but they are always of the cuddly, non-threatening, reassuring-type of story with a lovely happy ending – usually with the child/teddy/bear in question falling asleep very happily.

And yes, I know vampires are very popular but remember you are writing for 3–4-year-olds. Again the concept of having your neck bitten and your blood sucked out (albeit by some improbably beautiful person with perfect teeth!) is not going to make a young child feel particularly safe.

UNHEALTHY FOOD

Yes, you guessed it, the PC police have now outlawed fattening food being shown to children. Although I can't really believe we'll never see another picture book featuring a cake or an ice cream, it's probably better to avoid describing your characters eating hamburgers or chips or pizza or any other fattening 'junk' food. Let them eat . . . carrots!

OTHER UNSUITABLE SUBJECTS

I've already covered plenty of unsuitable subject matter but just to add a few more no-go subjects:

◆ Drugs, drug-dealing or drug taking.
◆ People taking medicine.
◆ Characters having piercings or tattoos.
◆ Smoking.
◆ Characters drinking alcohol or getting drunk.
◆ Sex, sex aids, nudity and descriptions of sexual organs – including anything that could be interpreted as suggestive, such as a young character sitting on a man's knee.
◆ Bullying – unless handled in a very sensitive and gentle way.
◆ And, as already discussed – bananas!

Remember I am talking children's picture books here. If you want to write gritty stuff, up your age group.

RHYME

Don't use rhyme. However brilliant your story, however clever your command of the poetic, your publisher will have great difficulty in selling your work abroad. This is because the tricks and devices used by poets, such as alliteration, onomatopoeia and the rhyming sounds themselves, will be lost in translation.

Obviously there are exceptions to this rule but only if you're already a big name or the current Poet Laureate (or your story is so incredibly strong that the lack of rhyme will not diminish it one iota).

I must add that occasionally rhyming texts can be sought after and you can always check with an editor or a publisher's website before submitting your text. But in general please be aware that it's unusual for a rhyming text to be commissioned from an unknown author.

HUMOROUS

It's quite risky being funny or making jokes in your text. This applies particularly to UK writers. British humour does not translate to the rest of the world since, apparently, nobody understands our sarcasm, irony or witticisms.

Punning, and any other clever word play which endows a piece of writing with multiple meanings, also falls flat on its face in translation.

But don't despair – if you write a lovely story that 3–4-year-olds and their parents will love it will probably, as a matter of course, possess an inbuilt gentle humour without you even needing to add any more on purpose.

WACKY STUFF

Nobody likes wacky either, which is very unfortunate in my case as nearly all my picture books are on the wacky side. What I mean by wacky is jokey stories that poke fun at the reader, or where the characters, and the things they do, are just plain silly. Or they have a kind of whimsical ridiculousness.

Whimsical ridiculousness is fine if it's gentle, as in *Winnie the Pooh*, but not if it's hard-edged or knowing or acerbic. Just remember you are not indulging yourself – you are writing for young children.

So to sum up this chapter – when an editor tells you they want something 'edgy and different' what they really mean is please play it very, very safe.

> **NOTE** The problems of using rude words, slang and dialect are all covered in Chapter 8.

Word count 6

WHAT IS WORD COUNT?

Word count just means number of words. In Microsoft Word 97–2001, you can find out your total document word count by simply clicking Tools, Word Count. In Word 2009 and later, the word count should be displayed on the Status Bar at the bottom of the screen.

You can also find out how many words a particular section of your document contains by highlighting the text in question and, for Word 97–2001, following the directions as described above. (In Word 2009 and later, this should appear on the Status Bar as the number of words in the selection.)

WHAT IS THE PERFECT WORD COUNT?

As already discussed, most picture book texts are somewhere between 150 and 500 words *in total*. From beginning to end. Actually I would say that, to be on the safe side and to give yourself the best chance of success, you should really limit your word count to 400 at the most.

From my own experience I know it is very tempting to ramble on and on, especially when you're caught up in an exciting plot, but the format of a picture book simply won't take a much wordier story. It's the pictures which are supposed to take up most of the physical space in the book, not the text.

Besides, most parents who are reading their little darlings a book before bedtime are so shattered and so desperate for at least five minutes of downtime they'll be picking a short one. Nobody wants to read their kids *War and Peace*! Publishers know this and therefore they all tend to reject work which arrives looking more like a novel than a picture book.

If you go back to Chapter 1 for a minute and look at the picture book layout you'll see that you generally have from page 6 to page 29 (24 pages) in which to write your story. Two or three sentences ×24 is going to give you approximately 400 words to play with at the very most. Furthermore, most picture books contain a number of pages with the text blown up large, which limits the number of words you can use. So ideally your 400 will need to come down even further to allow for this.

Why should some pages contain very little text? Well, to begin with, a varied word count makes each page less uniform and therefore more visually interesting. Next, it creates room for bigger pictures. And lastly, with a small number of words on a page, the publisher can choose a larger font. A larger font equals more impact. If you look at lots of picture books you'll see exactly what I mean.

So, to recap, aim for 400 words. If you can write a great story in, say, 300 words or even less you'll find yourself in demand.

> **NOTE** For those of you who are thinking '300 words! I can't get it below 3,000!' read on.

CUTTING WORD COUNT

For those of you who struggle to keep your picture book stories under 1,000 words, let alone 400, cutting word count is going to be difficult. You're not alone – the vast majority of picture book writers end up chopping chunks off their texts and it sometimes takes them years to get it just right.

In fact, if you find your writing to be on the wordy side, I would recommend you deliberately concentrate on getting your stories down on paper and worry about word count later. But at some point, the chopping will have to begin.

If it helps, remind yourself that the language of a picture book is simple. There are no long, involved sentences and very little description since the action is always shown in the illustrations.

So, for example, if you've written a sentence like this:

Jenny threw on her sandals, grabbed the key which was underneath the mat, flung open the

door and scampered past the deciduous trees and
pretty pink rose bushes which had just come into
bloom, down to the very bottom of the garden
without noticing Blue Penguin clinging for dear
life to her back.

consider making it more 'picture book friendly' and just
say:

Jenny was in such a hurry she didn't notice Blue
Penguin on her back.

Can you see how all the unnecessary detail (which would
make for boring illustration), such as the child putting
on her shoes, reaching under the mat and opening the
door, has been eliminated?

Other unnecessary text has also been cut, such as
the description of the garden which will be up to the
illustrator to describe in pictures. You do not need to
describe the surroundings in your text.

Also, an unnecessarily complex word – deciduous – has
been eliminated.

Overall you have now reduced 54 words down to 15
with no loss of meaning. In fact it's more dramatic and
far more illustratable now. A good result.

This may have been a rather extreme example but,
if your text is still languishing at 850 words, it probably does contain more than a few overlong or
over-descriptive sentences.

So examine your text for ways to reduce it. Be ruthless. Shorten and simplify sentences. Cut unnecessary description. Take out anything that would make a boring picture. Even shortening a catch-phrase that occurs throughout the text will save words.

Word count reduction is hard work and might take you hours and hours and many rewrites before you achieve perfection. But nobody said writing a picture book was easy!

7 *Plot planning and the rule of three*

PLOT PLANNING

It's easy to see when your word count is too high. What's more complicated, however, is working out whether your *plot* is too long or too short. By 'too long' or 'too short' I mean the *amount of story*. This is very important because a picture book text has to fit a very specific framework.

If your story is brilliant but contains too many twists and turns to fit the format it will be rejected by the publisher. And the converse is also true. If nothing very much happens, if there aren't enough illustratable scenes to fill the book, then that's equally pointless as far as a publisher is concerned.

> **NOTE** Don't for one minute think that a publisher will say 'Hey, we love your story but please add another 15 interesting scenes'. They'll just send a rejection.

So how do you know if you're in the right ballpark?

If you go back to my picture book layout plan in Chapter 1 you will see you have 12 double-page spreads to work with (i.e. 24 pages). One very good tried-and-tested method you can use to see whether your story will 'fit' the picture book format is to try to visualise what is happening in the pictures on each spread.

There are several ways you can do this:

◆ The first is to make up your own dummy book and sketch out (or describe in words) what is happening on each spread. This is time-consuming and only recommended if you don't have anything else to do with the rest of your life other than mess about with bits of paper and staples.
◆ On the other hand, you can use my layout plan and turn it into a brilliant plot planner.

To illustrate exactly what I mean, I am going to use the well known story *Goldilocks and the Three Bears* as my example. I will insert *Goldilocks* into my plot-planner layout plan and see what happens (see Figure 2 opposite).

> **NOTE** I have physically *written* the a very basic description of the plot on the layout plan simply because I cannot draw for toffee. But if it helps you, feel free to sketch in your action instead.

Can you see that *Goldilocks and the Three Bears* actually fits quite nicely into a picture book format? But what if it didn't?

Let's say you were the author of *Goldilocks* and were using my layout plan to see whether it contained the right amount of plot for a picture book.

If by page 29 you had only just reached the middle of your story, it would be obvious you had *too much plot* to fit the format. For example, let's say your Goldilocks' sat-nav was playing up and she found herself lost in the forest so she went for a little swim in the river, got chased by crocodiles, was abducted by aliens and, in order to escape, broke into the Three Bears' house, smashed their chairs, gobbled their porridge, wandered upstairs and, in recompense for the damage she'd done, spent three weeks decorating Baby Bear's bedroom before the entire house was blown down by the Big Bad Wolf . . . you could quite clearly see that your work had too many twists and turns to fit the format. It would have *too much* illustratable action. Too much plot. In fact it would be more like a novel than a picture book!

If, on the other hand, your Goldilocks was being chased into the sunset by the returning bears as early as page 15, you'd know you needed to write more. And by 'more' I don't mean padding. I mean, more interesting, illustratable story. More scenes. More plot. Still remembering you need to stick to the 400 words or so maximum word count.

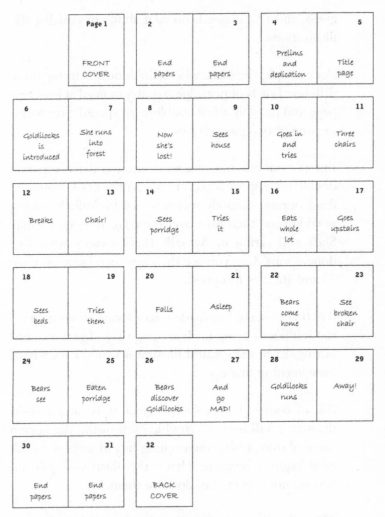

Page 1	2	3	4	5
FRONT COVER	End papers	End papers	Prelims and dedication	Title page

6	7	8	9	10	11
Goldilocks is introduced	She runs into forest	Now she's lost!	Sees house	Goes in and tries	Three chairs

12	13	14	15	16	17
Breaks	Chair!	Sees porridge	Tries it	Eats whole lot	Goes upstairs

18	19	20	21	22	23
Sees beds	Tries them	Falls	Asleep	Bears come home	See broken chair

24	25	26	27	28	29
Bears see	Eaten porridge	Bears discover Goldilocks	And go MAD!	Goldilocks runs	Away!

30	31	32
End papers	End papers	BACK COVER

Figure 2. Plot planner using *Goldilocks and the Three Bears.*

How long should each individual scene be?

This is impossible to say. But with practise and common sense, you'll find it easier and easier to make an educated guess, and a lot depends on your ability to visualise the illustrations.

For example, the scene where Goldilocks is trying three different bowls of porridge is going to need at least one page and possibly a full double-page spread. So allocating one or two pages is OK.

But if you ran that scene over, say, three separate double-page spreads (i.e. six pages) the book would be dead boring. Nobody wants to see Goldilocks eating porridge and then turn over the page and guess what? She's still eating it. Actually that's exactly what I've done. Oops! Can you see the page turn between page 15 and 16? Not too good.

Another mistake I've made is to allocate an entire page to Goldilocks going upstairs (page 17). Again it's dead boring. Even the greatest illustrator would have a hard time livening that up.

But of course, *Goldilocks* is a great story, and a good illustrator will have no trouble minimising the boring bits and maximising the exciting bits in ways you can't even begin to imagine. That is the illustrator's job and you are not expected to do it for them.

The point I'm making is that, by using this technique, you can see how well your story fits the format and whether it has enough (or not enough) meat on its bones to make an interesting and enjoyable book.

If you want to practise then why not take another fairly tale and have a go. I'm sure you can improve on my *Goldilocks* example too.

> **NOTE** You don't even need to use a nicely drawn-out plan like mine (not that it's anywhere near perfect). Just draw 12 large, numbered boxes on a piece of paper. And use a pencil because you can then rub out the bits you want to change and re-jig it without having to redraw a new plan every time.

So to recap: while you are planning and writing your picture book, and especially before you submit any work to a publisher or agent, check your plot length and try to ensure every single line of text moves the plot along.

While you're at it, try to imagine your illustrator sitting down and working on your book. Will they have lots of amazing things to draw or is your plotline uneventful and your characters boring? This may sound a bit harsh but it really does help to put yourself in the shoes of the illustrator when trying to improve your story, even if it means a painful rewrite.

THE RULE OF THREE

There are a number of 'devices' that are often used to improve the plot of a fiction story, the best known of which is the 'rule of three'. This hinges on the fact that three is the smallest number that can really establish a pattern which can be recognised by everyone.

If you read children's literature, including picture book fiction, take note of how many times the number three rears its head. For example, how many houses does the Big Bad Wolf attempt to blow down? And how many Billy Goats Gruff are there? How many bears live in the Three Bears' house? How many Blind Mice are there? How many times does Jack climb the beanstalk? Yes, you guessed it, three times.

So, if you plan to give your character one or two difficult obstacles to overcome, go a little further and give them three. If your character is going to attempt to do something, let them succeed at the third attempt. If a 'baddy' in your book is going to misbehave, let them get their comeuppance on the third occasion.

If you think about it, three attempts is quite a sensible number. Other than establishing a pattern, one or two attempts at success from your protagonist would be far too easy. On the other hand, five or six attempts could become boring and repetitive and, anyway, the length of your plot is restricted by the picture book format so a large number of attempts is fairly unworkable.

The rule of three can also be used as a textural device to jazz up your text. 'Up, up and away' is far more interesting than the boring 'Up and away'.

Even politicians use the number three to their advantage. What about Abraham Lincoln's Gettysburg

Address which spoke about 'of the people, by the people, for the people', or Julius Caesar's 'Friends, Romans, Countrymen', to name just a few examples. If they can do it, so can you.

8 Language and language structure

LANGUAGE STRUCTURE – HOW SIMPLE TO PITCH IT

Little kids need easy, simple language so, in general, avoid using difficult words and long, complex sentences. Remember you are writing for the 3–5-year-old. So a sentence like this:

> Once there were three diminutive squirrels who resided in a quercus tree at the heart of a deciduous woodland, constructing their dreys high in the branches.

is really quite unsuitable for a picture book text. The words 'diminutive', 'deciduous', 'quercus' and 'dreys' are all far too complex for the average 3-year-old to understand (and many adults too):

> Once there were three little squirrels who built their nest at the very top of a tall oak tree.

is much better.

Of course you might argue that using a more complex adjective to describe the squirrels' size, and that using the Latin name for an oak tree and the correct term for a squirrel's nest is highly educational. And you might also argue that the use of the word 'deciduous' might encourage a child into all sorts of discussions about which sort of trees shed their leaves and which ones don't . . . *but this is not the point.*

The fact is you are writing a children's picture book not an educational textbook. You are writing to entertain, to engage and to delight and nothing very much more. The real purpose of each sentence is to move the story along. The first example doesn't actually do that; it just waffles on trying to be clever and eloquent and articulate without actually achieving very much.

By far the best way to gauge language level is to read as many good picture books as you can.

This is not to say that a few interesting or colourful words cannot be included, but only if it's pertinent to the story and allows the general meaning and flow of the book to continue *without* the adult who is reading to the child having to break off mid-sentence in order to drive down to the shops to buy a dictionary!

Assuming the appropriate tone and voice

By tone I mean the attitude or manner of the narrator's voice – the voice you hear in your head as you read the story. Here are a couple of examples and the way they could be interpreted by the reader:

> Alex was a little boy.

This is fine. It's gentle. It's factual. Nobody can object to it. Now let's see a rather more unpleasant tone being used.

> Alex was pathetically short.

In this example the author (or the narrator in your head) has just poured scorn on the character and informed the reader of his stupidity by using the word 'pathetically'. This is not acceptable in a picture book text and neither is the next example:

> Alex had little, fat, hairy legs. He really should have taken his shorts to the charity shop and bought himself a pair of nice long trousers instead.

Now I quite like this because (I think) it's funny, but again it's an entirely inappropriate tone to use in a picture book. Not only does it poke fun at the character but it also employs the word 'should' which immediately makes you feel that the narrator is arrogant and bossy. Not very nice.

I think that, if you love children, if you respect them and care about them, then the tone of voice you use in your writing will naturally be completely appropriate.

The basic rule here is: *treat your audience with respect and don't talk down to them.*

To get a better flavour of how to speak to children through your writing, go and borrow lots of picture books from the library and read them with the narrator's tone of voice and style in mind. You will quickly see how gentle and even loving it usually is.

And please do not concern yourself with 'voice'. By this I mean the particular style of your writing that makes your work instantly recognisable to the general public. This can take many years and a filing cabinet full of rejections to mature, so there is little point worrying about it.

FIRST, SECOND OR THIRD PERSON?

Most picture books are told in the 'third person'. This means your narrator is using the words 'he', 'she', 'they' or 'it' (or a character's name) when describing what is going on in the story. Here are some examples:

- Alex was a little boy.
- They got caught in the storm.
- A larger monster had never been seen before.
- The wind blew the ship further and further from the shore.

Rather more unusual in a picture book is the use of the 'first person' narrative. This is where the narrator speaks about themselves and describes action (and feelings) from their own personal point of view by using the words 'I' and 'me':

- I am four years old and I have a million freckles.
- My brother's name is Peter.
- Tiddles is my cat and he loves it when I cuddle him.
- Mum and I went to the swimming pool yesterday.

Even more unusual for a picture book text is the use of the 'second person'. This is where the narrator speaks to the reader directly. For example:

- You get out of bed and take a shower.
- You are feeling sleepy.

Sometimes the first and second person can become almost interchangeable. You'll often find a mixture of 'you' and 'I' in a non-fiction book where the author's voice is chatty and conversational. This book is a good example. First and second person are also used extensively in adult fiction.

There is nothing to stop you experimenting with first and second person, just be aware that for picture books, third person is more common and probably safer.

WHAT ABOUT THE ACTUAL LANGUAGE?

As to whether it's best to write in English, French, Spanish, etc. – I'd say just write in your own language (or, more accurately, the language of the country where your target publisher's offices are located). That's a very long-winded way of saying if you live in the UK and you're submitting manuscripts to British publishers, write in English.

WHAT ABOUT FOREIGN TRANSLATIONS?

If your book is bought by co-edition publishers and sold in different countries it will need to be translated. This is good because, if for no other reason, your mum will be able to boast to everyone at the bus stop that her little darling has been 'translated into 25 languages' which is certainly very impressive.

Another advantage is that the more publishers who buy the rights to publish your book in their own countries, the more sales you will achieve overall and therefore the friendlier your original publisher will become. Plus, if a publisher who bought the rights to sell your book in, say, Mexico, subsequently enjoys wonderful success with it they'll probably be very keen to buy your next book as well.

> ***NOTE*** British English, Australian English and American English are considered different languages by publishers. Therefore a book that originates in the UK will need to be translated for the Australian and US markets. You would be amazed at just how much text has to be changed. More on this coming up.

From a technical standpoint, the way a foreign translation of a book works is that the actual printing and production occur at the same time for all the co-edition partners, whether the books are destined for the UK or China or even the moon! The printing presses churn out however many thousand books in, say, English, then somebody clicks a button and the next couple of thousand roll off the press in French. The illustrations remain the same, it's just the text on the page that changes.

All you really need to know about translation into foreign languages is that:

◆ co-edition sales are a good thing; and
◆ your publisher will sort all that out on your behalf.

DIFFERENCES IN SPELLING

It goes without saying that the spelling of every single word in your submission to the publisher (covering letter, title sheet and actual text) should be 100 per cent accurate – and if it isn't then your story will most probably be considered unprofessional and amateurish. But this isn't what I'm talking about here. This section covers the differences in spelling from one country to another where the basic mother language is similar (e.g. British English and American English).

There are literally hundreds of words which are spelt differently in the UK and the USA. Here are some examples of words you might want to use in a picture book:

UK spelling	US spelling
Centre	Center
Colour	Color
Daydream	Day-dream

Favourite	Favorite
Grey	Gray
Harbour	Harbor
Mum	Mom
Mummy	Mommy
Neighbour	Neighbor
Pyjamas	Pajamas

My advice is, don't worry about it. *Use the correct spelling for your home country* and leave any translation changes to the publisher.

DIFFERENT WORDS FOR THE SAME THING

Instead of just differences in spelling, many words will be completely different yet mean the same thing. Here are some examples that might crop up in a children's book:

UK word	**US equivalent**
Carrycot	Baby carrier
Crib	Bassinet
Camp bed	Cot
Cot	Crib
Curtains	Drapes
Dummy (baby's)	Pacifier
Holiday	Vacation
Jumper	Sweater
Nappy	Diaper
Post box	Mail box
Water pistol	Squirt gun
Wellingtons	Rubber boots
State school	Public school

Tea time	Late afternoon
Sweet	Dessert
Sweets	Candy
Squash	Cordial
Shopping trolley	Shopping cart
Rubbish	Trash
Paddling pool	Wading pool
Petrol	Gas
Lucky dip	Grab bag

I could continue for ever. My advice is, don't worry about it. Use the correct word for your home country and leave any changes applicable to future co-edition books to the publisher.

BE AWARE OF IDIOMS AND COMMON EXPRESSIONS

Well I could list a huge number here, but I won't. A few examples will suffice:

UK expression	US equivalent
Do a moonlight flit	Sneak out at night
Knickers in a twist	Hissy fit
Ten a penny	Dime a dozen

Again I would say, don't worry about it. Use the correct expression for your country and leave any changes applicable to, say, an American co-edition to the publisher.

Having said that, you must be careful about using too many localised expressions or area-specific dialects which cannot be easily translated. Always endeavour to use plain, simple language; after all you are writing for very young children and the most important thing is the story anyway, not the flamboyance of the language.

So, for example, instead of saying somebody was 'a dab hand at' (which may be translated to 'a crackerjack at' in the USA), just say the character was 'very good' at whatever it was.

You also need to consider that a UK expression that has an equivalent in the USA may have no equivalent at all in China, or Israel or Russia, which will not make your book very attractive to overseas publishers since they will have great difficulty translating your words. So be careful and keep it simple.

This discussion on language leads me nicely to a couple of things you may want to avoid.

RUDE WORDS AND SLANG

First of all, never use any sort of obscenity in a children's picture book. Your editor will be highly offended and chuck your text on the rejection pile.

Gentler rude words, such as bum, willy, snot, wee, poo, etc., are also pretty much off limits. There *are* books out there with this sort of vocabulary, and even a very famous picture book all about poo, but if you want to sell your work it's best to avoid it.

Remember that, in general, parents want to calm their kids down when reading a bedtime story. They don't want them rolling around on the floor laughing and then going to nursery school next day and talking about their willy to the teacher! You get the picture! If you absolutely must use rude words in your work become a children's poet.

As far as slang is concerned, I suggest you buy a good slang dictionary to check out words and topics for double meanings and entendres, so that you can avoid them.

> **NOTE** Rhyme, and whether to use it or not in your picture book, is covered in Chapter 5.

Spicing up and enhancing your text 9

SPICING UP YOUR TEXT

Now this sounds like I'm about to help you write a bodice-ripper novel, but actually this chapter is all about using little tricks-of-the-trade to make your work more visual and therefore easier to illustrate, not to mention more interesting for the reader.

Your illustrator will be the person who visualises your story and turns it into a series of pictures. The illustrator, probably alongside an art director or designer, will also be responsible for the design element of your book. But you can give yourself a much better chance of getting your work accepted if your text has great visual impact.

Note that I am *not* talking about instructing the illustrator to insert a flap or a peep hole or a pop-up at a specific point in your story. That sort of thing is down to the design team, not you. (Novelty books are discussed briefly right at the beginning of this book in the Introduction.)

Instead I am going to show you one or two ways to help your illustrator and to impress your potential publisher with the clever use of text positioning and choice of words.

Here are some ideas for you to try:

♦ Examine your story carefully. Using the layout plan given in Chapter 1, try to visualise what is happening on each of your 24 pages (from page 6 to 29). This is a good technique because it forces you to examine your text and plot in minute detail. Delete any 'boring' bits (as described in Chapter 7) and concentrate on creating visually interesting scenes for the illustrator to draw.

♦ Vary the amount of text you use in different parts of your story. Although I have recommended you try to keep your word count around 400 or so words, this doesn't mean using exactly 16.6 words on every single page. Use more words in some places and fewer in others.

♦ Use very minimal text for particularly dramatic moments. Minimal text also allows the designer to blow up those words hugely, which will create great visual impact. You can do this with, say, three or four words; you can't do it with five sentences.

♦ Use lovely descriptive sentences that an illustrator would find a joy to illustrate (and even the most inexperienced and unimaginative editor will be able to visualise). For example: 'When ladies have babies they get fat!' 'Bigger and bigger and bigger'; 'A huge SPLASH!' 'The boat toppled over the waterfall.'

- Repetition of individual words is good. In the second example given above ('Bigger and bigger and bigger') you will probably find the illustrator increases the font size on the repeated words to create visual interest.

- Repetition of phrases can also be very satisfying for the reader. Remember children love to join in and, if you give them a *chorus* or repeated refrain, they will be able to do just that. If you examine lots of successful picture books you'll see just how many of them make use of repetition.

- Use words that could lend themselves to being 'decorated' or printed in a fancy font to give visual appeal. For example, 'SPLASH! WHOOSH! HELP!'

- Visual appeal can also be given to descriptive words. For example, 'curly', 'wavy', 'twist'.

- Include some dialogue between your characters. Dialogue increases interest and changes the appearance of text on the page.

- Ensure your text doesn't just describe what you imagine is in the pictures. 'Lulu's teddy whooshed up, up and away' is good. The illustrator will immediately imagine a windy day with tree branches thrust sideways and leaves flying all over the place, teddy up in the air and a windswept Lulu looking terribly distraught.

However, 'Lulu's turquoise teddy was blown away by the wind in ever-increasing spiralling circles' is *too* descriptive. The illustrator will decide what colour Lulu's teddy is and how the wind is going to twirl the poor thing around, not you.

CREATING PAGE TURNERS

Try to create page-turners. By this I mean endings to sentences that make the reader want to turn the page and find out what happens next. Words such as 'until' and 'but' or phrases like 'and saw' or 'and then' or 'Oh no it's a . . .' all have the potential for being placed on a right-hand page so that the reader is forced to turn over the page to discover exactly what your character is shouting 'Oh no it's a . . .' about.

Writers of older children's fiction use this technique at the end of chapters, as do novelists. TV soap writers do it at the end of every episode. Whatever you like to call it, a page turner or a cliffhanger, with a picture book you can do it every few sentences.

One method is to use a smattering of sentences which can be split up in the middle, particularly at dramatic moments. This will give the illustrator the opportunity to create multiple pictures, or at least a choice as to which particular visual image they wish to illustrate. For example:

> Lulu's teddy whooshed up and up, and then down, down, into the lake. SPLASH!

The 'up' section of the sentence will make for a very exciting picture, and the 'down' section also has great potential for an entirely new scene, possibly with a page turn in the middle.

Basically what I am trying to do is encourage you to deconstruct your work line by line to see how it could be interpreted and visualised and therefore improved and made more saleable.

COMPANION AUDIO CDS

A lot of picture book publishers have now started to produce audio CDs and cassette tapes to sell alongside the printed version of their books. This concept lends itself nicely to stories containing songs, chanting, choruses or counting with which a young child can be encouraged to join in.

It's very useful, as an author, to be aware of this new development when writing your picture book text. Is there anything in your story which would lend itself to a more 'interactive' experience for the parent and child? I'm sure reading a bedtime story to a young child and listening to music and singing a song at the same time would be absolutely lovely.

Some audio CDs include a narrator reading the story aloud. Remember this when submitting work. How interesting or exciting is your story? How would it sound if somebody was reading it aloud? *'Poppy swam across the crocodile-infested river,'* or *'Poppy looked for the television remote control'.* See what I mean?

An even newer development is the emergence of the 'enhanced' ebook.

ENHANCED EBOOKS

In the past, the only choice a publisher had was whether to produce a new book in a hardback or a printed paperback version, or both. But now, virtually all publishers market their products in print *and* electronic form. If you go online to buy a picture book you will generally be given a choice of product to buy; print or ebook.

Virtually any hard copy book can be turned into an ebook, and picture books are no exception. But instead of simply reproducing the entire book in electronic form, with all the text and illustration fixed and static exactly as they appear in the print version, a new trend is for picture book publishers to attempt to add some value to the original text. I think this will happen more and more in the future.

'Enhancing' a picture book for the ebook market is primarily done to make the product more saleable (and more enjoyable for the reader). What I'm talking about here is animation, video, interactive components, sound effects, music, text which becomes highlighted as the narrator speaks, and even alternative endings!

ENHANCING YOUR TEXT FOR THE EBOOK MARKET

All of the things mentioned above (animation, video, interactive components and sound effects etc.) are time-consuming and costly to produce so not every publisher will do this, and most will wait until they see how the sales are going before they spend any money.

Having said that, to make your book even more attractive to a commissioning editor it's a good idea to think about whether your story has reasonable potential to be adapted and 'enhanced' as described above. Your editor probably will be on the lookout for stories with this sort of potential, so why not give them what they want!

Whether the reader will access sound and visual effects by clicking a button or tapping on a screen isn't your concern; that's the job of the technical production team. Your job as author is to look critically at your text and ask yourself the following questions:

♦ Is my story full of action or is it completely static?
♦ How much movement is there?
♦ What are my characters doing – climbing mountains or sitting still?
♦ What happens in my story that could become a sound effect?

One could almost say that the perfect children's picture book text of the future needs to possess the potential to become an audio CD or video game, albeit for a very young audience. Personally I'm a little horrified at the thought of picture book stories that include video, or that make all the sound effects instead of you or your child having to bother, and tell you exactly when to turn over the page.

In my opinion, nothing beats a real live book that you can hold in your hand and read to your child – the perfect bonding experience. But a book that reads itself? Now there's a thought!

10 *Editing*

Editing means reading and re-reading your text and then changing it in order to improve it and keep it consistent. Why should you bother? Simply to make your text more saleable and reduce the number of rejections you receive through sloppy writing or sheer carelessness.

Many writing books and websites call the business of editing and rewriting 'polishing'. Whatever you choose to call it, it's time consuming and hard work but ultimately worthwhile.

Here are some ways to edit your text.

SPELLING, PUNCTUATION AND GRAMMAR

Warning! Here comes the lecture about spelling, punctuation and grammar. Presumably, as you are reading this, you are serious about submitting your work but it is absolutely no good if the presentation of your material is unprofessional. Your story could be the best thing since sliced bread. It could be fabulously well written, interesting, hilariously funny, commercial enough to sell on the international market and definitely worth any publisher's time and money to produce and promote – but none of that will matter one iota if what the publisher sees when they first open your envelope is a jumbled-up mess littered with spelling mistakes and grammatical inaccuracies.

The fact is, successful authors are professionals and what you produce has to look the part. If not, your work will simply be rejected immediately no matter how brilliant it is.

If it helps, think of your manuscript as a CV and take as much care with it as if you were applying for a job, which in fact you are – the job of picture book writer. Therefore your very first editing job is to read and reread your text and correct every single little mistake.

If in doubt use a dictionary, a spellchecker, refer to a book on grammar and punctuation or ask a friend with a decent standard of literacy to proofread.

> **NOTE** Remember to correct mistakes in your covering letter and title sheet too (these are discussed in Chapters 13 and 14).

BEING CONSISTENT

Consistency in a picture book (or any fiction book) is another necessity. You would be horrified at how many aspiring picture book writers begin a story using a character who behaves in a certain way, uses particular phrases or possesses a certain individual style, only to have them undergo a complete personality change a little later in the text.

For example, if your main character is described as short with seven brothers, it's incredibly sloppy to describe them later on as possessing the ability to reach the top shelf or include a scene in which they talk to their six sisters.

Inconsistency leads to confusion and, if you confuse the commissioning editor, your text will be rejected.

Luckily it isn't difficult to keep your characters and your story consistent throughout; after all, you are only writing a very short, simple book. Imagine how much more complicated it is for novelists churning out 500-page texts involving multiple characters!

When it comes to the characters, I'm assuming you have already made a long list of each one's attributes as suggested in Chapter 4.

So, for example, let's say you have created a character who is a four-year-old male panda bear with three brothers, who is very inquisitive and owns a pink elephant teddy bear that's always getting lost. Just make sure he has the same personality, the same behaviours, the same possessions, the same likes and dislikes and the same number of siblings of the same sex all the way through the book.

This may sound like basic advice but virtually all writers are guilty of the most ridiculous consistency mistakes. Only the most professional (and successful) actually do something about it.

Other things to look out for when reading a picture book text for consistency are as follows:

+ Are all your characters present and correct throughout the text? A protagonist doesn't usually disappear halfway through a book but I've seen texts from would-be authors in which they do.
+ Are place or character names the same throughout? Have you spelt your character names consistently throughout?
+ Is your writing style consistent? Rushing a book can often lead to a ponderous beginning and a breakneck pace later on as the writer gains confidence or simply becomes bored with the whole process and can't wait to finish.
+ Is your language structure similar throughout? I've seen texts that swing from the very formal to a mass of abbreviation and slang and back again. It's disconcerting for the reader because it feels like the author doesn't know what they're doing.
+ Have you stuck to the script and found a way for your protagonist to conquer their fears/solve their problem/succeed in their quest – or have you completely forgotten about your original plot?
+ Do your characters do and say things which are consistent with their ages or personalities? You can't describe a four-year-old character being put to bed

by their mummy one minute and dancing in a night-club the next!

◆ Have you switched viewpoint halfway through or used a different tense for no good reason?

◆ Do you use any repeated phrases or choruses which, once they've got going nicely, suddenly disappear for several pages or change completely?

◆ Have you suddenly started rhyming your text half-way through? This is a very common consistency mistake.

These sort of mistakes indicate a sloppy, unprofessional attitude to your work, so always spend time checking.

REWRITING

So what do you do when you've reread your work and found it wanting? Simple, you change or improve it. It may be:

◆ basic spelling mistakes you are correcting;

◆ rewriting due to the discovery of inconsistencies in your plot line or writing style;

◆ rewriting due to the discovery that your plot is too short, or there's simply too much of it and you've got to work out what to take out; and/or

◆ substituting new characters or changing their gender because you've written a story with a male protag-onist but have just heard a particular publisher is looking for stories about girls.

Whatever your reason, sometimes it can take years before you're satisfied enough to send your work out; I have 38 different versions of *Stop, Elephant, Stop!* on my computer and they're just the ones I kept. Sometimes picture book authors make so many changes to their texts it might have been better if they'd attempted a full-length novel instead!

Just ensure that, when you edit your text, you keep a copy of the old version on your computer just in case you labour away all day long only to then decide that you've ruined it. This is easily done by giving your new version a new name or adding a number ('Stop, Elephant Stop! Version 95') or adding the current date to the filename.

Also, don't rewrite just for the sake of it (unless you're enjoying yourself). Remember, your goal is to finish the manuscript and send it to publishers, not work on it for a lifetime.

11 *Titles*

CHOOSING A TITLE

You need a title which will be featured on your manuscript submission and in your covering letter to the editor (and on your computer so you can find it should an editor call you up and ask you to email another copy). However, in my experience, no matter how brilliant your title is, somebody somewhere will change it.

But anyway, back to how to choose the original title before the editors get to change it. First read your story and see if you can condense the main plot into one sentence. To do this it helps to be very clear about what your story actually describes.

If it's about a boy who wants to grow you might call it, as I did, *Growing Alex* (my publisher later changed it to *You'll Soon Grow, Alex*). If it's about a little girl whose tummy rumbles a lot then you might call it *Isabel's Noisy Tummy*, as David McKee did.

MAKING YOUR TITLE INTRIGUING

These are very descriptive titles, but descriptive titles don't always work. For example, if you were writing a book about some jungle animals who jump into a water hole to cool down, as I did, you might think of calling it *Animals Get Hot in the Jungle*. But that would be dead boring.

Another possibility would be to call it *Elephant Jumps into the Waterhole* or *Elephant Jumps*. The problem here is you would have given your punch line away.

Far better to call it *Stop, Elephant, Stop!* This sounds exciting and a bit mysterious and it does make you wonder what on earth Elephant does that makes everyone scream 'Stop!'

Remember that your title will be glanced at by a potential buyer in a bookshop or online and needs immediately to intrigue and interest them, over and above any other book.

You can, if you're very clever, try to think up a title which will appeal to the adult buying the book. *Guess How Much I Love You* is an excellent example. Every parent wants to tell their child how much they love them and, even better, also wants to encourage their child to express their love for them.

> **NOTE** The cleverest title will not disguise a poorly written, boring or otherwise unsuitable book. Better to submit a brilliant book with a silly title than submit a text that doesn't live up to its promise.

General advice for titles is as follows:

* Keep them fairly short (so the font used can be blown up large and people can see it across a shop floor).
* Keep them simple.
* Keep them interesting and a little mysterious.
* Don't give away your punch line.
* Make sure nobody else has used it before (see below).

IS MY TITLE UNIQUE?

It's best if your manuscript has a unique title – you don't want to be pitching a story that the editor thinks could have been already published by somebody else. Luckily it's easy to find out if your proposed title has ever been used before: simply type it into a search engine or the search bar of an Internet bookshop like Amazon.

If your title turns out either to have been used already or to be very similar to another book you'll just have to go back to the drawing board.

Preparing your manuscript

12

PICTURE BOOK MANUSCRIPTS – A REAL-LIFE EXAMPLE

When you send work to a publisher you will need to send three things:

1. The actual manuscript itself.

2. A title sheet, which is physically attached to the manuscript.

3. A covering letter which basically introduces you and your work to the commissioning editor.

This chapter covers the presentation of the actual manuscript itself and how to prepare it properly, but to begin with I will show you the manuscript of my picture book, *Stop, Elephant, Stop!*, exactly as it was originally sent out to publishers.

From this example you will see how to set out your story on the page and also how to split the sentences.

STOP, ELEPHANT, STOP!

Spread 1
It was a burning hot day on the grassy savannah. Too hot to sit in the burning sun. Too hot to sit in the sizzling shade. Too hot to do anything except . . .

'Have a nice cold bath,' laughed lizard, and he jumped . . .

Spread 2
. . . into the water hole with a tincy-wincy splash.

'OOO that looks nice,' sniggered stork. 'I think I'll have a bath too.'

Spread 3
And in jumped stork with an ever so slightly bigger splash.

'OOO that looks nice,' giggled gazelle. 'I think I'll have a bath too.'

Spread 4
And in jumped gazelle with a right in the middle size splash.

'OOO that looks nice,' zapped zebra. 'I think I'll have a bath too.'

Spread 5
And in jumped zebra with an even bigger look at me splash.

'OOO that looks nice,' tittered tiger. 'I think I'll have a bath too.'

Spread 6
And in jumped tiger with a huge I can do better than that splash.

'OOO that looks nice,' joked giraffe. 'I think I'll have a bath too,'

Spread 7
And in jumped giraffe with a massive you've never seen anything like this before splash.

'OOO that looks nice,' panted elephant. 'I think I'll have a bath too.'

Spread 8
Stop!' shouted all the animals. 'Stop Elephant STOP!'

Spread 9
But elephant was too busy charging . . .

Spread 10
. . . towards the water hole to hear them.

Spread 11

And in he jumped with an absolutely amazingly gigantic I'm better than all of you put together SPLASH!

Spread 12

'Hey!' panted elephant. 'Who pulled the plug out?'

(Wide-angle shot of the empty water hole, and all the dripping wet animals standing there looking very cross with elephant.)

THE END

Andrea Shavick

(My contact details went here.)

NOTE As mentioned above (but please forgive me for repeating myself), this text is copyrighted which means you cannot copy it or tweak it and send it to a publisher under your own name. I am including it purely to illustrate how a text should be presented on the page.

NOTE You may have noticed that my story has 'spread numbers' included. This is not always recommended – see 'Spread numbers – are they necessary?' below.

Now for the ground rules on formatting and page set-up.

PAPER SIZE, ORIENTATION AND QUALITY

The paper size needs to be A4, orientation portrait.

Use clean white paper. Normal copy paper is OK – you don't need to buy expensive watermarked paper. And no fancy letterhead or pretty colours, just plain white will do.

FONT AND SPACING

For virtually all manuscripts I recommend you use the run-of-the-mill Times New Roman size 12 regular, or maybe Arial, if you prefer. Verdana is also easy on the eye.

When you initially prepare your page set-up, include large margins – at least 3 cm all the way round. This is so that, should the editor fall in love with your story, they can immediately start to scribble wonderful things about it in the margins.

It also needs to be double spaced so the editor has room to scribble even more wonderful stuff between the lines.

SPREAD NUMBERS – ARE THEY NECESSARY?

Generally it's best to avoid including spread numbers. They are included in my example manuscript for several reasons:

- First, the word count is small so I can get away with it. If my word count was very much longer, adding spread numbers would just extend the number of pages, and too many pages might be off-putting to an editor.
- This particular text lent itself well to spread numbers as it's fairly obvious where they should go. But this is not always the case.
- I also felt that, since there is so much repetition in the text, spread numbers would separate my sentences better.

If in doubt, don't include them.

WHEN TO BEGIN A NEW LINE OF TEXT

The general rule is:

- every time a character speaks; and
- where you feel that a page needs to be turned.

For example:

It was a burning hot day on the grassy savannah. Too hot to sit in the burning sun. Too hot to sit in the sizzling shade. Too hot to do anything except . . .

'Have a nice cold bath,' laughed lizard, and he jumped . . . into the water hole with a tincy-wincy splash.

I have shown this example without spread numbers. You'll see the first three and a half sentences run on nicely together – it feels natural. They all make up the introduction, so to speak, and therefore will be included on the same page. So no need to begin a new paragraph.

But then you get to 'except' which is a natural time to put in a page break. Think about where the pages should turn and keep your audience wondering what happens next.

At this point Lizard begins speaking. All speech requires a new paragraph.

Then the text runs 'and he jumped . . .' which is a lovely place to break the line because you can see this is yet another natural page turn. I wanted 'into the water hole with a tincy-wincy splash' to be given a page all to itself.

This is how to split the sentences on the page. Once you become familiar with lots of picture books you'll notice sentences being split over several pages all the time.

Just ensure the split makes sense. Don't say 'It was a burning hot day on the . . .' because it doesn't work. How is your illustrator going to illustrate that? Split your sentences where you can add tension and interest, not just for the sake of it.

Remember, you are not writing an essay. You are not writing a letter. You are not writing a report. You are writing a picture book text.

PAGINATION

Pagination means, in printer speak, page numbers.

Personally I recommend you number the pages of your manuscript but not the title sheet or covering letter. Page 1 should be the first page of the actual text.

Keep page numbers as unobtrusive as possible by placing them, ideally, in the header or footer.

CONTACT DETAILS

Your name and address and contact details, including telephone number and email address, should be printed on the title page, at the end of the text and in the covering letter. It is not necessary to plaster your details over every page of your manuscript.

However, I'd still recommend you include your name and the title of your story on every page, just in case the editor reading your manuscript chucks it on a pile of other people's work. Silly to be rejected because the three most exciting pages of your text have been mislaid!

Placing your name, title and page number in a 'header' or 'footer' looks neat and, especially if you keep them small, has the advantage of not distracting a reader from the main text.

PRINTING OR HANDWRITING?

Any text you send to a publisher must be printed. Do not send handwritten texts. Handwriting went out with the ark. And if you don't have a computer and printer – buy one!

All publishers require authors to be computer literate. If and when you become a successful author you will do virtually all your communicating with editors via email. It's probably quite difficult to do that if you have to go to the library or an Internet café every time you want to send a message.

Do I say 'the end' at the end?

Yes. Editors are not stupid, but it helps to have something to separate the actual manuscript text from your contact details.

13 *Title sheets*

THE TITLE SHEET – A TRIED-AND-TESTED EXAMPLE

As already mentioned, you need to send three things to the publisher – the manuscript, the title sheet and a covering letter.

The title sheet (see page 103) is just an A4 sheet of plain paper that is attached to the first page of your manuscript which carries the title of the story, your name and contact details, a very brief synopsis of the story and possibly some other information, such as word count.

STOP, ELEPHANT, STOP!

by

ANDREA SHAVICK

Address, telephone number and email address go
here

It's a burning hot day on the grassy savannah.

All the animals enjoy cooling off . . .
until Elephant decides to join in
the fun . . .

240 words (some illustration ideas
in italics)

ARE TITLE SHEETS NECESSARY?

Yes. A book has a cover – why not give your manuscript one? Besides, if an editor likes your story they'll pass it along to other members of the editorial team to read, but they're unlikely to pass along your original covering letter. Therefore a title sheet, which remains firmly attached to the manuscript, is the only way your work can be easily identified as yours. Besides, including a title sheet gives your work just that extra little bit of professionalism.

The title sheet doesn't have to be fancy. The example given here is simple but effective. You can use it as a template for all your manuscripts.

If you want to jazz it up a little then you might consider varying the fonts used for the title, but it's not really necessary. Editors are not interested in your prowess with Word Art.

As for the word count – I always include this unless it's particularly high, in which case I normally develop acute amnesia and leave it out!

If you feel so inclined you can include the copyright symbol © next to your name (find this in Word by going to Insert and then Symbols), but it's not really necessary. You already own copyright (for more information, read Chapter 18).

The covering letter

14

THE COVERING LETTER – A TRIED-AND-TESTED EXAMPLE

When you send out your manuscript to a publisher, alongside the actual manuscript with its title sheet attached you should also send a covering letter. This is a businesslike letter addressed personally to the commissioning editor.

Its purpose is threefold:

1. By addressing your covering letter to a specific editor it's likely your manuscript will land on their desk, instead of the general submissions pile along with everyone else's work.

2. Your covering letter will introduce yourself, explain a little bit about your story and, hopefully, induce the editor to read it immediately.

3. Including a businesslike letter with your submission is impressive and professional – and not many people do it.

Use the example letter given below as a template for your own covering letters; just amend it to suit yourself.

> **NOTE** The covering letter here is an actual tried-and-tested template I have used for many of my initial covering letters to publishers where I am sending them unsolicited manuscripts. It works! 'Unsolicited' means sending the manuscript to a publisher in the hope that they will like it enough to buy it and turn it into a book (i.e. I am sending it out 'on spec').

Name of editor
Editor title (e.g. Commissioning Editor) Children's Books
Company name
Address   date

Dear Ms XYZ

I enclose a picture book text which I hope you will be able to consider.

Stop, Elephant, Stop! is written for children of approximately 2–4 years of age. It's a fun story which describes a burning hot day on the grassy savannah. All the animals are having a lovely time cooling off in the water hole . . . but then Elephant decides to join in the fun.

Thank you in advance for reading my work and I do hope you enjoy this story. I look forward to hearing from you as any feedback you can give me will be most valuable. I also have a number of other manuscripts available should you wish to see more of my work.

Thank you for your time.

Best wishes

Andrea Shavick

Your address

Tel
Mobile
Email address

ARE COVERING LETTERS NECESSARY?

Yes. As already explained, the covering letter is the means to introduce yourself and your manuscript in a pleasant and businesslike way. It doesn't have to be long winded. You are not expected to tell the editor your life story and if you did they wouldn't be interested. The whole point is to impress them with your professionalism and to persuade them to read your text.

You will see that in my example covering letter I sum up the plot of *Stop, Elephant, Stop!* in just a few lines.

Summing up your story plot in such a way as to make it sound interesting and without giving the plot away completely is actually very difficult. It takes practise and authors often spend almost as long on the synopsis as writing the entire text itself. But it's worth the time and trouble as this is your one chance to 'sell' the book to the publisher. Snappy, interesting and concise is what you're aiming for and, if you can add that little bit of mystery, then even better.

And why should you bother with a synopsis? Well, if your book is accepted for publication you'll be expected to write the back cover blurb anyway, so why not start now?

MENTIONING PREVIOUS WORK

My example covering letter is very short and to the point, but if there is anything pertinent to say you can include a line or two about your previous writing history. Obviously if you haven't got anything published previously, don't say anything (although I would normally say something to the effect of 'If you like my style of writing please just ask and I will be delighted to send you a number of alternative texts' – assuming you've got some to send, of course).

WHAT NOT TO SAY IN THE COVERING LETTER

Never say things such as the following:

♦ My children/grandchildren love it.
♦ It's not very good but . . .
♦ It's only been rejected 15 times.
♦ It's better than anything in the shops right now.
♦ I wrote this 35 years ago but was too scared to send it to a publisher . . . until now.
♦ I've always wanted to be an author, it's my dream job.
♦ All my friends think I'm a terrific writer.
♦ Writing was my best subject at school.
♦ How much will you pay me?
♦ I am prepared to sell it to you for £100K.
♦ I deserve a chance.
♦ My dog just died.
♦ I need some good luck for a change.
♦ I need to pay off my mortgage.
♦ It's much better than anything you've published before.
♦ I'll contribute to the cost of publishing it.

OK, so these examples are a little extreme – but actually editors see things like this all the time.

Much better to be businesslike and to the point. Talking about your grandchildren or apologising or using any of the silly phrases listed above simply marks you as an amateur. And saying that writing 'is your dream' or using that terribly hackneyed phrase 'I really, really want it' is also cringe-worthy. You're submitting a manuscript to a publisher not auditioning for the *X Factor*! Think of it as applying for a job – the job of writer.

ADDRESSING THE LETTER

Just ring up the publishing house and ask for the name of the commissioning editor for picture books. Or look on their website – usually somewhere under the heading of 'manuscript submissions' you'll find a name or a department to send your work to. Of course, you may be instructed to address incoming mail simply to 'The Editor' and, if so, then that's all you can do.

However, if you are lucky enough to be given a name, ensure you spell it, and the person's title, correctly. If in doubt, ask the receptionist to spell it out for you. This is very important – a wrongly addressed letter or the editor's name full of typos just shows you to be slapdash and unprofessional.

> **NOTE** Commissioning editors and virtually everyone else who works in the publishing business invariably have impressive titles. But don't be misled: 'Publisher' or 'Editor' doesn't necessarily mean they own the joint. Having said that, editorial staff are nearly always pleasant, friendly and helpful, so treat them courteously.

Illustrations

15

SHOULD I SEND PICTURES WITH MY MANUSCRIPT?

If you are writing picture books do *not* send any pictures to the publisher. This includes your own drawings, copies of anyone else's work, ClipArt, illustrations from existing books or photos cut out of magazines. Far better just to say in your covering letter that, if they decide to publish your story, you'll be more than happy to work with one of their illustrators, and leave it at that. If the publishing house likes your text *they* will choose the illustrator.

I should also point out that, if the publishing house falls head over heels with your text but absolutely hates the unprofessional pictures you've sent, you may receive a rejection simply because the editor in question doesn't want to upset you.

Even if you are a wildly famous writer, you'll hardly ever get a choice of illustrator. All you can do is hope they pick an illustrator you like.

Even being given a choice doesn't usually work. Here's the usual scenario:

1. Your publisher asks you to suggest an illustrator for your work.

2. You visit every bookshop and library within a 100-mile radius researching illustration style.

3. After six months of this you finally come up with the perfect man/woman for the job and triumphantly inform your publisher . . .

4. who immediately picks somebody else!

I promise you, this is what happens. But your publisher isn't really trying to upset you or give you false hope – they're actually trying to pick your brains. They do have some interest in how you visualise your work.

Anyway, all I'm saying is don't put any effort whatsoever into finding yourself an illustrator. If you want to visit a million bookshops that's fine, but maybe use the time productively and read the picture book *texts* to hone your own story-writing skills.

Speaking of illustrators, if the publisher picks a famous one then be warned. Some of them are known for demanding the lion's share of the royalties. Totally unfair, but that's life.

WHAT IF I DON'T LIKE THE CHOSEN ILLUSTRATOR'S STYLE?

Pretend you do. I'm being serious. Do not get labelled 'difficult'.

WHAT IF I AM AN ILLUSTRATOR?

Ah, then that's different. What I should have said was 'If you are writing picture books do not send any pictures *unless* you are a professional illustrator'.

If you are a professional illustrator then definitely mention this in your covering letter. If you can provide a listing of the work you've had published and maybe include some examples of your work, even better.

> **NOTE** Never send original artwork.

In fact many publishers actively seek out children's authors who can also illustrate their own work. The reasons for this are simple:

- ◆ It's easier to negotiate contracts with just one person.
- ◆ There's no chance of any misunderstandings arising between author and illustrator. And no arguments about what the illustrations should look like.
- ◆ Only one person to send proofs and party invitations to.
- ◆ Only one person to deal with in regard to book design, text changes, illustration ideas, etc.

◆ An author/illustrator has skills that could be utilised elsewhere (e.g. to illustrate another author's work).
◆ Publishers might be able to get away with paying less to one person, as opposed to two. This is probably the main reason.

So to reiterate. Do *not* send pictures or photos or any sort of illustration material unless you are a trained professional or, at the very least, possess a degree in illustration. And that includes drawings your best friend has cooked up, your children have painted or your own cut-and-pasted efforts however cutting edge you think they may be.

ISN'T THERE ANYTHING I CAN SAY ABOUT THE PICTURES?

You can give very brief illustration suggestions (in *italics*) on the right-hand side of the text itself, like this:

'Yippee! This is fun,' giggled Wendy.   (*she's flying*)

But you have to be brief and only do it where it really is impossible for the publisher to imagine what's happening from the given text, and it certainly isn't acceptable to do it more than once or twice.

A better alternative is to provide some general illustration suggestions at the bottom of your text, such as this example taken from my original submitted text of *Stop, Elephant, Stop!*:

Elephant jumped . . .   'Here I go!'
                               into the water hole.

'Hey!' panted Elephant.   'Who pulled the plug
                               out?'

(The animals are in the water hole, wet and bedraggled, and all the water has been splashed away.)

I included the illustration suggestion at the bottom because I felt that, without it, the punch-line was not immediately obvious.

However, with a line like this (taken from my *The Truth About Babies*):

When ladies have babies they get FAT.

anyone reading it will be able to imagine a very fat, pregnant lady, maybe even a cartoony lady with a massively fat bump. It's so obvious, illustration instructions are not required.

> **NOTE** It's important to say that, although your picture book will be illustrated, the text should always be good enough ('strong enough' in publisher speak) to stand on its own two feet without you explaining what is going on.

Interestingly, the pictures you imagine in your head while writing a picture book story may never really match up to the pictures your future illustrator will create. The most likely scenario is that the imagination of the illustrator is far superior to yours, and that's fantastic.

Choosing a publisher 16

WHERE SHOULD I SEND MY MANUSCRIPT?

Sending out a manuscript to the wrong publisher is one of the most common mistakes new writers make.

It is vital to send your manuscript to publishers who might be interested in your work, *otherwise you will have absolutely no chance whatsoever of having your work accepted.* By this I mean publishers who produce books of the same genre as the work you are producing.

In other words, if you write picture book fiction, *only send your manuscript submissions to picture book publishers.* Do not send your work to a non-fiction publisher, do not send it to one who churns out romantic novels and do not send it to one who specialises in humorous gift books. You need a picture book publisher.

This advice may seem blindingly obvious and I apologise if you are now wondering why I am treating you like a complete imbecile, but I assure you that commissioning editors receive the wrong type of manuscript every single day, and every single time all the poorly targeted manuscripts are thrown in the bin. If you were an editor producing, let's say, children's non-fiction, and you found yourself bombarded by picture book manuscripts, you'd throw them away too.

Why do people do it? Here are some reasons authors send their work to publishers who do not produce the same genre of book. Because:

◆ They think that a publisher who doesn't normally touch children's books will surely change their entire company policy once they've read their story.
◆ They've seen the name featured in the bestseller charts.
◆ They are trying to avoid the competition (i.e. the thousands of other picture book writers trying to get noticed).

Whatever the reason, it won't work.

If you want to get published you must do your homework and research the book market before you send out your manuscript. There are thousands of publishers out there and, unless you plan to submit work to all of them, you must give some thought as to which ones could provide an appropriate home for your work.

However, before you can make any decisions as to where to send your work you need to be clear about exactly what you are actually offering. Although these may seem like obvious questions, you need to examine your work and ask yourself:

- ◆ What is my genre? Is it fantasy, animal character, humour, fairytale, true-to-life, adventure, etc?
- ◆ What is my target age group? Is it toddler, 3–4 years, 4–5, infant, junior, etc.?
- ◆ Is my story a stand-alone picture book story or could it fit readily into a specific, existing series?

What I am getting at here is to encourage you to think of your story as a product. Not a story about what happened to you or your children or something you feel intensely emotional about, or even a wonderful and creative product of your imagination, but a product. A product just like a pair of knickers or a tin of baked beans on the supermarket shelf. If you can do that then it will be easier to tackle the job of selling your story to a publisher, and the right publisher, in a businesslike way.

To use a very crude analogy, if you were a baked-bean manufacturer then it would be a pointless waste of time to try to sell your product to cake shops. If you send your picture book to the wrong type of publisher that is exactly what you will be doing.

IDENTIFYING SUITABLE PUBLISHERS

You need to identify publishers who are currently producing similar material to yours because these are the organisations who are most likely to be interested in your work. To find out what is currently being produced by specific publishers you can do some, or all, of the following:

- Spend time perusing bookshops, especially those which offer a good range of the type of book you have written. Smaller bookshops can often be more rewarding in terms of research than the big high-street names which often carry only the most mainstream bestsellers or Disney products.
- Visit your local library. Libraries are a wonderful source of good research. Also, the children's librarian can often tell you what sort of subjects are in fashion and which books, and authors, are the most popular. Some libraries have larger children's departments than others so you may have to travel.
- Research your subject and genre through the library catalogue; usually this is available online.
- Research as above, but via the big online bookshops, such as **www.amazon.co.uk** and **www.amazon.com**.
- Look at publisher websites. They all list their current offerings and many list forthcoming books (and they'll often state their policy on submitted material).
- Borrow from your library (or buy via my website at **www.shavick.com**) the latest copy of the *Writers' and Artists' Yearbook*, or the *Children's Writers' and Artists' Yearbook*, or the *Children's Writer's and Illustrator's Market UK* (see my recommended list at the end of the book).
- For those of you outside the UK, just look for the local versions of these directory books on Amazon.

You can also ring up publishers and ask them to post you their catalogues (ask for the one that includes children's picture books). They'll usually do this free of charge.

NOTE To find out who publishes a specific book, either look up the publisher information in the book's online listing (in say, Amazon) or simply search inside the book itself until you find the verso page which will list publisher information (including their address). The verso page is normally situated opposite the title page but could be elsewhere or even on the back cover. Just look for the small print.

Aim to find a handful of possible publishers to send your work to initially – remember you are looking for those companies who are currently producing work similar to yours.

The next chapter discusses the nitty-gritty of actually sending out your work.

17 Submitting work

I have already explained how to prepare your manuscript and identify suitable publishers – this chapter covers the minutiae of physically sending out your work.

HOW MUCH TEXT SHOULD I SUBMIT?

For children's picture book stories – and in fact for all children's stories less than approximately 6,000 words or so – *send out the entire text*. Do not send half a story. Do not send three sentences. Do not send a note promising the editor that they will be amazed by your brilliance and your telephone number (yes, it's horrific but plenty of people do exactly this). Send the whole caboodle.

Remember to put in the envelope:

◆ The text (manuscript) itself.
◆ The title page attached to the text itself.
◆ A covering letter addressed to the specific editor which introduces yourself and your work and persuades them to drop everything else and read it.

Should I include a stamped, addressed envelope?

Yes. Enclose an SAE (a large envelope with return postage). If you do not, they will never reply. This is *very* important.

In fact, if a publisher absolutely loves your work they are much more likely to email you or ring you up, but you must still give them the option of writing you a letter.

Besides, even if you receive a rejection, it's still preferable to be told so (and sometimes you will get extremely valuable feedback at the same time). With no SAE you'll never hear from them again.

What about postage?

Put the correct postage on the letter containing your manuscript. If it doesn't have enough stamps, the publisher will *not* go to collect it from the sorting office or mail collection depot. Neither will they pay for delivery of the manuscript the next day. Why should they?

If you are in the UK, check the postage carefully as there are new rules on letter size and new pricing structures to go with them, but this applies wherever you live. If in doubt, take your envelope to a post office and get it measured and weighed.

WHAT ABOUT RECORDED DELIVERY?

If you are prepared to pay more money then you can use Recorded Delivery. My apologies to those of you in the USA and anywhere else outside the UK – Recorded Delivery is a UK postal service whereby the person or company to whom the letter is addressed is required to give a signature on delivery (and it costs more than normal post).

However, unless the mail in your area is particularly unreliable, my recommendation is simply to use the normal mail service.

HOW SHOULD I FASTEN IT ALL TOGETHER?

A lot of waffle is written about how to keep all the pages of a manuscript together, and personally I would say if there is more than one sheet then just staple it together neatly. I have heard people say you should use paper-clips or put your work in a binder, and I once heard somebody recommending you tie it all up with pretty ribbons – but that really isn't necessary. One staple will do.

Having said that, the covering letter should really be separate and not physically attached to the text.

WHY CAN'T I JUST EMAIL MY TEXT?

At this point you are probably thinking, why can't I just email my story to the editor in question? Why bother with all this printing and envelope stuffing and schlepping down to the post office to get it weighed and correctly stamped?

Email is obviously a vital tool, and if you secure a publishing contract your publisher will correspond with you by email virtually all the time. However, when you are initially submitting work it's still preferable to post a hard copy, and here's why:

♦ Editors may be more inclined to read your work if you submit a hard copy – many editors take home interesting-looking manuscripts to read in the bath or on the train and they can't do that with your emailed submission unless they print it all out, and that involves effort, paper and time. A printed manuscript is there 'on a plate'.
♦ Many publishers only accept hard-copy manuscripts.
♦ Getting hold of a commissioning editor's name is reasonably easy, obtaining their personal email address is not. And it's pointless emailing your text to the publisher's 'customer services'.
♦ Even if you manage to find out the commissioning editor's personal email address they are most unlikely to open any document sent as an attachment. Would you open an attachment that came from an unknown source?

Having said that, if the publisher, or their receptionist or the commissioning editor themselves, provides you with an email address you can certainly send your work to it. But beware, emails are very easy to delete. All your hard work in the junk box. My personal experience is that email submissions are useless unless you know the editor personally. Having said that, the following questions and answers may prove useful.

WITH EMAIL, DO I STILL NEED A COVERING LETTER?

Yes. Although you can shorten it a little. This should be inserted in the body copy of the email that you send to the editor.

Ms Adele Smithson Commissioning Editor
Company name

Dear Ms Smithson

I am attaching two picture book texts which I hope you will be able to consider.

The Elephant Mum describes the things nobody tells you about when your mum is pregnant, together with some of the smelliest and most awful things to expect from a new baby brother or sister.

Monster Homework is about how two little boys from different planets get together to do their homework, making a few surprising discoveries in the process.

Thank you in advance for reading my work and I do hope you enjoy these stories. I look forward to hearing from you as any feedback you can give me will be most valuable.

Best wishes

(Your name here)

(Your address, telephone number, mobile number and email address here)

WHAT PROGRAM SHOULD I USE FOR THE ATTACHMENT?

You can normally send your manuscript as a Word document attachment to your email. Actually, I would always check the format the publisher will accept email submissions in. They may prefer a completely different format altogether. Best to ring and ask.

They may prefer you paste your story into the email and not send your work as an attachment at all.

One of the publishers I worked with only accepted documents in Rich Text which was incredibly annoying as it deleted all the formatting I had so carefully prepared. Just one more reason why I prefer hard copy.

> **NOTE** When sending an attachment ensure the document name is targeted to the correct publisher (e.g. 'Shavick picture book story for Penguin). You don't want the editor to find an attachment in their email box called 'picture book story 95th try' or, even worse, with the wrong publisher's name!

HOW MANY MANUSCRIPTS CAN I SEND AT THE SAME TIME?

I think the same answer is correct for either postal or email submissions. One, two or three at the most. I'm talking about *different* manuscripts submitted to the *same* publisher here (assuming you have more than one text to send).

HOW MANY PUBLISHERS CAN I APPROACH SIMULTANEOUSLY?

Ah now this is interesting. Most publishers would say just one primarily because, although they're quite happy to keep you waiting months before bothering to reply, they'd absolutely hate a rival firm to be offered your story before them.

Most successful authors, on the other hand, submit work to three or four, or even more. The truth is that if you are going to wait for a children's book publisher to reply before sending your story out to the next one on the list you'll be 90 before you get anything accepted.

In the very unlikely event that two different publishers make you an offer for your manuscript at the same time you can always do the following:

◆ Get yourself an agent who will set up an auction or bidding war depending on how attractive a proposition your manuscript is.
◆ Buy a (very) big bottle of champagne. Believe me, this is not a problem.

> **NOTE** Some publishing companies are owned by other, larger publishing companies. Should you send your manuscript to two different publishing houses using the same address? Why not? I can't see you have anything to lose.

I'VE SUBMITTED MY MANUSCRIPT — NOW WHAT?

A number of things:

♦ **Write more stories.** As I've already explained, nobody will publish a one-trick pony. Unless you have more stories to sell or more work on the go, nobody will take you seriously. Besides, many editors, having read a story they rather like, will immediately ask the author for other examples of their work. You cannot say well . . . err I haven't written anything else, or that will be the end of your glittering publishing career.

♦ **Keep records.** Make sure you know which story has been sent to which publisher and when. This may involve a little filing of your work on your computer. If somebody likes your work they may ask you to email it either to them or to a more senior editor and if that happens you need to find it quickly. Another reason to keep good records is that, if you update a story, or tailor-make it for a specific publisher's requirements, you can identify which version you sent. Authors often have multiple versions of each story – often different lengths, or with different endings, etc. You probably will too, once you get going. If you use a PC then just open a folder in Windows Explorer and call it BOOKS. Inside BOOKS you can then open separate folders for each title you write. That way you can easily keep multiple versions of the same title together.

◆ **Lastly, and by no means, least – enjoy your life.** Do not stay at home waiting for the phone to ring. No agent or publisher has been known to ring an author in the entire history of the world while said author was sitting by the telephone. Just make sure your email works.

OTHER SUBMISSION ADVICE

For more help than you can ever possibly use, simply search the Internet for 'writer's resources' or 'submitting manuscripts', etc. Although watch out as much of the advice isn't offered by experienced, published authors.

Copyright – how to protect your ideas

18

WHAT IS COPYRIGHT?

Copyright is an area of great confusion. Many new writers worry about what they have to do to protect their copyright and, even more importantly, how to prevent another writer waltzing off with their ideas. Although copyright is a complicated issue, I will try to simplify it a little.

The main thing to know is that you *cannot* copyright an idea or an outline of a story plot, or even a title. So let's say you came up with a plotline (obviously this is not a picture book!) which involved the school life of a teenage wizard-in-training and his pursuit by some evil creature who is continually trying to kill him. There would be nothing to prevent another writer using your idea and developing it into a full, seven-part blockbuster. Your basic idea, however unique or genuine, cannot be protected. It's simply too vague and really exists only in the realms of the imagination.

Things change, however, when your text is physically written down, either on paper or computer file or recorded on disc or tape. By this act, copyright, and the right to be identified as the author of the work (called 'moral rights'), is automatically acquired.

There isn't anything else you need to do. By writing or typing or recording your story it automatically belongs to you and you alone. This applies whether or not the work is published or unpublished.

Having said that, there are some steps you can consider taking to protect your copyright and to prevent people stealing your ideas.

How to protect copyright

The best advice I can give you is not to send a manuscript anywhere unless:

◆ You have kept an identical copy at home and a note of where and when and to whom you sent it.
◆ You have ensured your name and contact details are clearly marked on the text.
◆ You only send your work out to reputable publishers and agents.

Of course it goes without saying that you should never send out any original illustrations.

Some people recommend that you should also print your picture book text out, put it in an envelope and mail it to yourself. When it arrives, assuming there is a clear date stamp on the envelope, keep the envelope unopened. If anyone subsequently pinches your story you will be able to prove *you* wrote it and exactly when.

Personally I wouldn't bother with this. To use your proof you will have to go to court. Better to put your energy into producing really good stories, sending them out to publishers and keeping a faithful record of what you sent to whom and when. The fact is that all publishers and agents are far too busy looking for good, saleable stories to forward the ones they *do* receive to other writers. They are usually only too pleased to find somebody capable of writing good stuff.

The other thing you might want to do to protect your copyright is to use the copyright symbol © next to your name on the manuscript whenever you send it out to publishers or agents. But it isn't really necessary – you already own the copyright simply by putting the work down on paper.

You could also consider only sending your manuscript to a named editor rather than a vague 'Commissioning Editor' but, again, if your manuscript is any good it will be read by all manner of folks.

No, mainstream, reputable publishers are not your enemy – it's the folks out there on the net who are the real baddies.

NOTE Ironically, a rejection from a publisher can also act as proof of ownership – so always keep rejections.

INTERNET PIRACY

The big spanner in the copyright works is the Internet. The Internet has led to an absolutely enormous increase in plagiarism (illegal lifting of another person's words and passing them off as your own). So do not post your most valuable unpublished work on the Internet, either on your own website or anyone else's.

I would also avoid Internet publishers and online writing magazines. Although there are some who are entirely reputable, many will attempt to persuade you to submit your work to them by tempting you with the vague promise that your unpublished work will be read by hundreds of publishers scouting for talent. If you allow this to happen you really are inviting the entire world to pinch your ideas.

Even published works can be plagiarised or copied once displayed online, as I have personally learnt to my cost. Unfortunately there are countless organisations who see nothing wrong in scanning, uploading and exploiting all manner of published works with the aim of selling on your title to an unsuspecting public, often in the form of an ebook.

Actually, individual people (i.e. the public) are not so innocent either. Once you become a successful children's author you'll find your work on the Internet all over the place being passed off as somebody else's work. And if you write children's poetry there'll be no end of people 'borrowing' your work without asking permission.

There are steps you can take to combat this kind of piracy but generally it's a little bit like trying to hold back a tsunami with a sandbag – the Internet is simply so huge there's little you can do.

In the UK the Society of Authors provides advice on copyright and 'moral rights' (as do many writing organisations around the world). Once you have a work accepted by a *bona fide* publisher you may need to consult them. For now – just get writing.

19 *Agents*

WHAT DO AGENTS DO?

Among other things, a literary agent will do the following:

- Sell your work to publishers.
- Negotiate contracts with publishers on your behalf.
- Sell subsidiary rights on your behalf (i.e. electronic, bookclub, translations, film).
- Give you literary advice (possibly).

As to whether you actually need one . . .

DO I NEED AN AGENT?

This is a popular question, partly fuelled by the popular press who seem utterly incapable of writing about successful authors without mentioning their literary agent and how said agent got them their first million-dollar book deal.

People also think that it must be easier to find an agent and let *them* have the hassle of selling your work than having to write to/email/telephone large numbers of publishers yourself. Which can be dead boring, tedious and time-consuming. How much better to sunbathe while the agent does all the work!

And, of course, who wouldn't want to be able to drop the words 'My agent' into a conversation when trying to impress one's friends or mum?

The answer is that you need a literary agent *only* if you are writing adult or teenage fiction. This is because the majority of publishers in these genres will discard work that arrives unsolicited. They will usually only consider work that has already been vetted and sifted and recommended by another professional in the business – e.g. a reputable literary agent.

If you are a picture book writer (and even if you are a writer of older children's fiction or non-fiction) then you will not necessarily need an agent. There are enough publishers out there who accept unsolicited manuscripts to last you a lifetime, and in any case if you are going to send your work to agents you might as well put your energy into sending it out to publishers.

THE DISADVANTAGES OF USING AN AGENT

Personally, I think there is nothing better than making contact with an editor and getting to know them and what they're looking for. When you have an agent you become one step removed from this personal interaction as all correspondence and communication will bypass you completely.

Obviously you may get to know the editor at a later stage, once their company has accepted your work, but with an agent you will never receive a letter or email directly from the publisher requesting you to send more texts, or giving interesting suggestions as to what to write about, or even rejecting your work but at the same time offering valuable feedback.

If you do decide to approach agents (listings of literary agents and their specialities can be found in *The Writers' and Artists' Yearbook* and by searching the Internet) ensure they take on children's work.

Also do not be put off by the unnecessarily rude manner in which many agents reject authors (more on rejections soon). The truth is most agents are wary about taking on unpublished authors and can be horribly dismissive if approached by one such person.

Of course, once you have a publisher trying to ram a contract down your throat you'll find virtually all literary agents suddenly become far more friendly and approachable. But if in doubt – don't bother.

Four more disadvantages to agents:

◆ They take a cut of your royalties – quite a large cut, maybe between 10 and 20 per cent.
◆ You could wait longer for your money since the publisher pays them and not you. Agents have been

known to go bust or simply be incredibly slow when it comes to settling accounts.

♦ All reputable, well established agents will have plenty of other clients, all of whom are better known and bring in more money than you do. This means they could pay you less attention and do less work for you than you might expect.

♦ Despite what they claim, many agents know next to nothing about the children's picture book market.

Have I put you off yet? To be fair, a good agent will be more than capable of negotiating a contract and might even be prepared to read all your fledgling works and give constructive feedback. However, I can assure you, the one thing virtually every author in possession of an agent does is complain about them!

NOTE Never give any money to an agent. Reputable agents will pay you, not the other way around.

20 *Your work is accepted – now what?*

WHAT WILL HAPPEN TO MY TEXT?

Probably nothing for several months. Why is this?

First of all, there may be huge numbers of unsolicited texts for the publisher to wade through before they get to yours. Secondly, when they eventually read your text and they like it, your story has only just begun its very long trek up the face of Everest. For not only must the initial reader love your text but the next person in the hierarchy will also have to read it and fall in love with it too, and then the next, and the next, and so on.

Children's editorial departments are full of people who all (usually) get along very well together and like to be involved with every project, and that includes your text on its tortuous journey from printed manuscript to real book.

That means everyone in the editorial department will read it, and sometimes they'll also take it home and read it to their own children or the children in the nursery school next door.

NOTE A 'reader' is a person employed by a publisher to read manuscripts and separate the wheat from the chaff, allowing editors to concentrate on other things.

The next person to be involved will be the art director, who will probably email or fax your text to a couple of potential illustrators to get some feedback.

What they'll be asking the illustrator is as follows:

◆ Do you like this text?
◆ Would you be interested in illustrating it and, if so, how much will you charge?
◆ Can you give us any idea of the sort of treatment or style concept you think would work best?
◆ Can you knock up some roughs before lunchtime? (Publishers want everything yesterday.)

Now your poor, long-suffering story has to jump through yet another hurdle. Will the illustrator like it enough to spend months working on it? I am sorry to say this, but even if the entire editorial department luuurve your work a disinterested or critical illustrator's reaction could kill your project stone dead.

But assuming they *do* like it and the editorial and art team approve the roughs they receive back, your text will probably then be discussed, talked about and argued over at an 'acquisitions' meeting. Your text might be officially accepted for publication at this point, but it's more likely to have to endure intricate examination all over again by the following publishing departments:

◆ The sales team (who will be asked if they think they can sell it to wholesalers and retailers).
◆ The rights team (who will be asked if they think they can sell it to overseas publishers).
◆ And lastly, but most importantly, the accountants who will decide in their wisdom whether they think your picture book story will sell enough copies to make the company money.

After all, as I have explained before, your lovingly written text is just a product and, in the end, it all comes down to the bottom line – profitability.

> **NOTE** Some publishers accept work very quickly; others take years to reach a final decision. And of course if they read your text and hate it then you'll get a rejection (on which more later).

My manuscript is being taken to a book fair: why?

One thing that is quite likely to happen is that the publisher will tell you they love your book but cannot offer you an actual contract until they have several overseas sales in the bag.

I think I should explain that a book fair is not an event attended by the general public; it's purely for the book trade. Bologna, London and Frankfurt are the main locations for book fairs in Europe but there are many more around the world.

Each fair is attended by publishers, the larger and more successful ones taking exhibitor space in which they display their new and forthcoming books. This is where the sales and rights people can normally be found, guzzling down cups of coffee while attempting to sell as many rights as they can (including, hopefully, your book) to publishers from other countries. Meanwhile, their acquisitions department (and buyers working for the large book retailers) will be trudging around the fair looking for interesting books to buy.

> **NOTE** 'Rights' is just publishing jargon for a contract given by one publisher to another, granting them the 'right' to publish a book in their own territory (i.e. the country in which they are located). For example, I originally sold my picture book, *You'll Soon Grow, Alex*, to Orchard Books in the UK, and they then sold the rights to an American company called Walker Books who subsequently published it in the USA under their own banner.

Anyway I digress. Having your book taken to a book fair can be very frustrating for an author because you've basically been told, on the one hand, 'We luuurve your text' and, on the other, 'We won't commit to anything before we've secured overseas sales'.

Again, it all comes down to the numbers. Remember I told you that your baby (I mean your text!) is just a product, no different from a can of baked beans or a pair of knickers? If you think of your text like that it will help you to understand why your publisher doesn't want to commit to paying you anything until they know it will sell.

Frankly I don't blame them. Too many books that don't sell equals financial disaster for the publishing house in question. So hopefully your book will sell in bucket-loads to publishers all the way around the globe and then your contract will arrive.

WHAT IF MY BOOK DOESN'T SELL?

If you are unlucky your book may not sell at the book fair, probably for no fault of the text itself. Maybe some other story is the sensation of the day; maybe the sales people leave your manuscript in the bottom of their briefcases. Who knows. But sometimes if there are no takers your potential picture book is once again dead in the water.

Having said that, if your publisher is really 'in love' with your text they may try again next time (one of my picture books travelled to three different book fairs before it sold). This is quite normal and the only disadvantage to you is that you will need to be very, very patient.

> **NOTE** American authors may be at an advantage
> here – the USA has a far larger potential
> market for book sales than, say, the UK,
> and therefore overseas deals may not be so
> critical to the viability of a book.

WILL MY STORY BE CHANGED?

Once your story is officially 'accepted' and you have a
contract with a publisher (more on this soon), you have,
in effect, sold it to them. It's theirs. Therefore they can
do whatever they want, and that includes changing your
words and the names of your characters.

This will not be done lightly but there may be good reasons (e.g. to make your text more understandable and/
or acceptable to a foreign audience). But there are almost
always changes made which you will know nothing about
until you're holding a copy of the book in your hand.

If that revelation has just made you gasp with horror
– self-publish! The only writers who can throw their
weight around and demand their precious words are
never altered one iota are those who already have a
track record of making their publishers a lot of money.

WHAT HAPPENS IF MY EDITOR LEAVES?

Unfortunately when you consider the staff turnover of
many publishers, this is quite likely to happen. There
are several outcomes to this scenario:

- ◆ The new editor will love your story and continue to represent you and push your story at sales and acquisition meetings.
- ◆ The new editor will hate your story and you'll find yourself in receipt of an apologetic rejection letter.
- ◆ The old editor loves your story so much they take it with them to their new job (assuming they're still going to be working for a company who publishes picture books).

All three have happened to me.

WHAT DO I DO ABOUT COPYRIGHT?

See Chapter 18 for the answer to this question.

WHAT IS AN OPTIONS CONTRACT?

Occasionally a publisher may really like your story but not be in a position to offer you a contract. An options contract allows a publisher to 'reserve' the right to buy your book without committing themselves immediately.

This once happened to me – the publisher in question (who shall remain nameless) loved my text but would only consider one specific illustrator. Unfortunately for me this illustrator was already committed to a whole series of other projects and had no idea when they might start work on my book. The publisher therefore asked me to sign an options contract.

There are all sorts of reasons why options contracts are offered but, basically, the author will receive a small amount of money in return for an undertaking not to offer the particular work to any other publisher for a specified time.

The downside to this is that:

◆ nothing happens with your text for a long time; and
◆ there is no guarantee that the publisher will ever use your work.

Despite the disadvantages, it's worth taking advice before refusing an options contract. I didn't. I reasoned that, since the publisher was desperate enough to offer an options contract in the first place, the story must be pretty good and therefore I would have no trouble selling it elsewhere. Silly me. I never sold it.

This is the thing about picture books. One publisher loves what the next one hates. And none of them knows what they really, really want until they see it.

WHERE CAN I OBTAIN CONTRACT ADVICE?

If you have a book accepted by a publisher and you live in the UK, join the Society of Authors. Their annual fee includes contract vetting and advice as well as a host of other advantages, information and events. If you live outside the UK just search the Internet for 'author societies' or 'writing organisations' to find your local equivalent.

It is unfortunately beyond the scope of this book for me to delve into contracts in any detail, but I don't really need to. Let your writing organisation do the work. Obviously if you have an agent they will negotiate your contract for you.

Whatever you do, don't become so deliriously happy about having a picture book accepted that you sign the first piece of paper the publisher sticks under your nose – always get advice, and negotiate.

ROYALTIES AND ADVANCES – HOW MUCH WILL I EARN?

Many publishers will pay you an 'advance'. This is money paid to you in advance of any sales. You may receive your advance upon delivery of the manuscript, but in the case of a picture book it's more likely to be forthcoming once contracts are signed. Not all publishers pay advances, and very few pay large ones (unless you're already a very successful author).

Royalties are different. A royalty is money paid to you *after* the book has been out in the shops for a while generating sales. Royalties are usually paid once or twice a year and the amount you'll receive depends on how well your book has performed in the marketplace and on the world stage. High sales and numerous foreign co-editions equals good royalties. Poor sales means virtually no royalty payments and a publisher who won't be very interested in your next work.

Furthermore, you won't receive any royalty payments until your book has earned out the advance (the advance being just that – an advance on royalty payments). Some books never earn out their advance, but at least you will never be required to hand it back.

Amounts of royalties vary, depending on your contract and how much you, or your agent, have been able to negotiate. Ten per cent net receipts is common – unfortunately so is 5 per cent or considerably less.

Often the 10 per cent is split between author and illustrator. This means you will receive 5 per cent (unless your illustrator is one of those who demand a bigger percentage of the takings than you). Furthermore, 'net' receipts can often mean the amount of money your publisher receives after they have paid all their costs and expenses, given huge discounts to the shops and negotiated ridiculously cheap deals with book clubs and sister companies in foreign lands.

As many picture book writers have discovered to their cost, a publisher selling what sounds like a huge number of books in some faraway country actually equates to a royalty not much bigger than the cost of a cup of tea! OK, I am exaggerating but 5 per cent does *not* mean you will get 5 per cent of the cover price of the book.

It is impossible to advise you on the exact amounts your writing will bring in as every contract, and every book's potential, is different. Some books make nothing. Some books make millions. All I can say is write for love, not for money.

WHAT IS A FLAT-FEE CONTRACT?

This is where the publisher pays you a fixed, one-off figure for the text and nothing else. You will not receive any royalties in the future. Is this a good idea?

Well, no it isn't if the publisher sells 25 million copies of your book. They will be very happy and you will be left kicking yourself. On the other hand, if your book manages little more than average sales your flat fee will appear more than generous.

Some picture book publishers only offer flat fees, but everything is negotiable, especially if they luuurve your story.

To conclude this section – if you are offered a flat fee, take advice from the Society of Authors or similar organisation in your own country *before* you sign a contract. If you can, try to negotiate even a small royalty after, let's say, a certain number of books have been sold. That way you can pocket the flat fee and still see some financial benefit should your book go on to outsell the Bible.

IS THERE SUCH THING AS A CANCELLATION FEE?

Yes, but only if there is one specified in your contract in the event of the book not being published.

WILL MY NAME BE PRINTED ON THE BOOK?

Yes – you are the author. There will be a copyright notice on the verso page and your name will appear on the cover and title page alongside the illustrator.

What is public lending right?

As an author you will be entitled to claim Public Lending Right (PLR). This is a tiny amount of money paid to authors every time one of their books is borrowed from a public library. Different countries have different schemes – your writing organisation will advise you.

The amount of money you will receive varies but is usually very small (e.g. a few pence or cents per book borrowed). But with enough borrowings from enough libraries you could be looking at fairly large annual payments. For many authors, PLR represents a larger revenue stream than their royalties so it's definitely worth joining up.

Another organisation, the Authors' Licensing and Collecting Society (ALCS), collects fees for photocopying and recital of works (e.g. when a book is photocopied in a school or when somebody reads your poem at a literary festival). This can bring in unexpected monies which is very welcome.

The Society of Authors or similar writing organisations will advise you.

Pseudonyms

A pseudonym, or pen name, or *nom de plume* is the author name that appears on your book, and it doesn't necessarily have to be your real one. Many famous writers have created different identities for their reading public (for example, Lewis Carroll, Mark Twain, George Orwell and Lemony Snicket).

Whereas most writers use their own names there's nothing to stop you choosing something else. You don't have to change your name legally.

There may be good reasons why you might want to choose a different writing identity:

♦ Your real name could be easily confused with another more established writer.
♦ Your real name is in common usage and you want to sound more distinctive or individual.
♦ You want to hide your identity, or change your sex, or present yourself in a different light.
♦ You are already an established writer of, say, gothic horror and don't want your young readers to find out!

Whatever you decide to do will remain between you and your publisher, but be warned. A wonderful new name will *not* persuade a publisher to buy your book if the story's no good – but it will provide you with a good excuse to waste a lot of time when you could be writing.

WILL MY BOOK BE PUBLISHED IN HARDBACK OR PAPERBACK?

Picture books used to published in hardback and, approximately a year later, in paperback. This is no longer the case. Economics now dictate that picture books are produced only in paperback – the exception being the rare book that sells millions, in which case your baby will be produced in paperback, hardback, BIG book, bath book, board book, miniature book and gift book alongside the character cuddly toys, films, DVDs, board games, T-shirts and maybe even as an 'adult' version!

How long before my book hits the shops?

Minimum 18 months, maximum . . . well my slowest book took five years. You will have to wait for a slot in the publishing schedule; you might also have to wait for an illustrator to become available. You might even have to wait for said illustrator to have a baby, bring it up and put it through university before they can find the time to work on your text!

Of course, as previously mentioned, you may also have to wait for your publisher to interest sufficient overseas co-edition partners before they commit to the actual print run and sometimes that can take years.

It seems that, if you want to be a picture book writer, you need *patience*.

21 *Dealing with rejections*

WHY IS WORK REJECTED?

Don't worry about rejections – even great writers receive hundreds. Think of each one as a stepping stone to your goal of being published. If you get upset every time you receive a rejection your skin isn't thick enough. Nobody ever, ever got their very first story accepted by the very first publisher they submitted it to.

A rejection doesn't necessarily mean your story isn't up to the mark either. There are plenty of other perfectly rational explanations:

♦ Your story, although good, isn't quite commercial enough (i.e. the publisher doesn't think they can make enough money selling it). That's perfectly reasonable. Publishers are not charities, they're businesses, and to stay viable they need to make a profit. It costs a fortune to buy, illustrate, print, promote and distribute a picture book, so profit margins are always going to be a major consideration.

- The publisher hasn't the resources to take on your book because they've just spent their entire budget buying a picture book story written by a pop star, actor, member of royalty, WAG or other such celebrity. Unfortunately, this is a frequent gripe of authors in all genres.
- Although the entire editorial team love your story, the accountant doesn't.
- It's a little too similar to something else they have in the pipeline or have already published previously.
- The publisher has no free space on their list. Publishers' scheduling and timetabling of forthcoming books is not dissimilar to a supermarket conveyor belt – maybe theirs is simply too overloaded at present.
- They've had to cut down on the number of books they publish due to economic and other belt-tightening reasons.
- The editor is about to waltz off to Bologna or some other book fair and hasn't got time to consider any new proposals.
- They can't think of a suitable illustrator.
- They *can* think of a suitable illustrator but said illustrator is too busy, has moved to Mars, has just given birth to triplets, has taken a three-year sabbatical or just doesn't fancy your book. Or they asked for too much money.
- Your story is unsuitable for that publisher – they just don't do books on death, ducks, dingbats . . . whatever. This is where research can save you a lot of trouble up front.
- The editor didn't bother to read it. Maybe they were too busy worrying about their sick goldfish or trying

to get their own picture book story accepted (now that's a very common problem for picture book writers – competing with the editor).

♦ They just don't recognise brilliant story writing when they see it. You only have to think about how many publishers rejected *Harry Potter* to realise this is a distinct possibility.

Also you must always remember that the likeability of a picture book story is entirely subjective. You may love a particular book, your best friend may hate it. See what I mean? A rejection could simply mean your writing doesn't rock that particular editor's boat. I was once told by a hugely successful children's writer with over 60 books to his name that he expected to sell only one in every 40 texts he pitched. One in 40! That means 39 rejections for each single success. The moral of this particular story is *don't give up*.

WHAT WILL THE REJECTION SAY?

All rejections from publishers will be polite. Editorial staff are usually very pleasant and don't enjoy hurting people's feelings.

However, many rejections will be totally impersonal or will simply explain that your story is not quite right for their list.

As to why they won't tell you the real reason for rejecting your work, well there are lots of explanations:

- They haven't got the time to write personal letters to all the picture book story authors who write in.
- They are too nice – unlike agents who will freely and gleefully tell you your work is rubbish and holds 'absolutely no interest for them whatsoever'. (Don't worry – it's not personal.)
- Because, for some perverse reason, a small proportion of picture book editors seem to enjoy telling you: 'We *loved* your book. The characters are so *sweet* and so *believable*. It made us *cry* with laughter. We've never seen anything so *brilliant* and so utterly *original*. We all rolled around on the floor in hysterics for *three whole hours* . . . but, hey, sorry it's not quite right for us.'

> **NOTE** Please don't email me accusing me of cynicism. I've had more than one rejection exactly like that.

GOOD REJECTIONS

Yes, they do exist. You will definitely find (assuming your work is reasonably good and well targeted to suitable publishers) that you begin to receive rejections that say something like:

> This story isn't suitable but we like your style – can you send us some more work?

If this happens, and especially if the rejection comes from a named editor and includes a direct telephone number, do not pass up such a golden opportunity.

Ring up the editor in question (I wouldn't recommend emailing, it's too impersonal), remind them who you are and the name of your story and what they said in their letter and try, if you can, to find out what they *are* looking for.

Of course they may not know. Most editors cannot describe the perfect text until it lands on their desk, but they may have particular likes and dislikes, the knowledge of which might prove invaluable to you.

At the very least, you will have begun building a relationship with them and, hopefully, secured their agreement for you to send work in future *directly to them*.

So don't be despondent if you get a rejection that says no, but we like your work, send more. A rejection like this is a brilliant opportunity to get your foot in the door. And if you haven't got any other work to send – get writing quickly!

WHAT IF I DON'T HEAR ANYTHING AT ALL?

This is very common. I recommend that, once you've sent off your manuscript, wait a month and then call up the company and ask very politely whether they know what's happening to your script. Be friendly. Remember they get hundreds, even thousands of manuscripts every week.

Some publishers will ask for your name and the title of your story and then tell you exactly where your text is in the scheme of things and even whose desk it is currently sitting on. Other publishers will just fob you off with

'We'll contact you if we're interested', which means they have no filing system and absolutely no idea.

Sometimes a publisher will call or email you to request you *resend* a story to them. I've had this happen to me several times and, on one occasion, the inquiry resulted in a sale. Amazing, considering the first time they read the manuscript they rejected it.

Maybe the topic just came back into fashion; maybe the editor's boss had just asked them to find a story about XYZ and they remembered reading mine. It can happen.

I'VE HAD 15 REJECTIONS: NOW WHAT?

How many times should you send out a text before you give up on it? Many experienced authors would say about ten times.

Even after ten rejections, don't discard your text completely. Change it. Rewrite it. Tweak it a little. Repackage it. Give it a new title. And then send it out again. Wait a few years and try again. If all else fails, you can always self-publish.

> **NOTE** Commissioning editors change their jobs more frequently than most people change their knickers so, if you got a rejection from a specific publisher and it's been sitting in your filing cabinet for a year, send it out again. The new editor might love it.

CRITIQUE COMPANIES AND OTHER FEEDBACK

If you have received a lot of rejections for a text (and even if you haven't), you can always consider paying a critique company to provide you with a professional appraisal. Many critique companies will provide you with a huge amount of truthful and constructive criticism as well as all sorts of ideas on how to improve and sell your work. But they will always be very careful how they choose their words.

The fact is that many people cannot stomach brutal criticism about what is, in effect, their cherished creation. For this reason many critique companies invariably present their views in a kind and quite gentle manner. There's nothing wrong with that but just be aware that no critique company will ever say 'This story is rubbish and will never get accepted by a publisher'.

There are some other ways you can obtain feedback:

◆ Ask your most honest friend with young children to read your stories to them and to give you their reactions.
◆ Ask somebody you absolutely trust to read your work. Ask – does the story make sense? Do they think the tone, language, plot, etc., are suitable for a young child? Are there inconsistencies in the story? Is your spelling, grammar and punctuation up to scratch? Does your story make them feel something (happy, sad, etc.) or does it bore them to tears?
◆ If you know any teachers you can ask whether they would be prepared to read your picture book stories

to the Reception children and tell you how they reacted. Don't worry about your text only being at the manuscript stage – a good story will always be capable of captivating an audience, with or without pictures.

Bear in mind that a personal friend or that teacher you know may do exactly as the critique companies do – temper their feedback so as to not upset you. Another problem with asking people you know is they'll often be *too* enthusiastic, probably because they like you. And that may be very flattering but it isn't helpful.

Lastly, I'm afraid you must accept that a rejection that comes from a publisher or an agent *is* feedback. They are saying no. But as you have seen from this chapter, a no doesn't mean a story is necessarily of poor quality or that your chances of selling it are low. It just means that you should:

- ◆ consider tweaking or improving it;
- ◆ send it out to other publishers; and
- ◆ think of it as one more step along the road to publication.

22 Other routes to publication

Although this book is primarily about picture book publishing, it's definitely worthwhile discussing, albeit briefly, some other areas of the market that you may want to consider, namely:

Longer children's fiction
Series fiction
Adult non-fiction
Freelance writing
Self-published printed books
Self-published ebooks
Vanity publishing
Online publishing

I hope the following short articles will give you some alternative ideas.

LONGER CHILDREN'S FICTION

You could try and write longer fiction – these are stories for older children (from 5 to 11 years) and teenagers.

They can be a little easier to sell than picture books because:

♦ The publisher doesn't have to factor in the high cost of professional illustration and colour print process-ing because most longer children's fiction has either black and white line drawings, or no illustration at all. This brings the price of production down and with it the risk factor for the publisher.
♦ Because of these reduced costs it's less likely that a publisher will be obligated to try and sell your book worldwide – most longer fiction is produced, at least initially, for the domestic market (i.e. just the coun-try in which the publisher operates).

Other advantages include not having to worry too much about language or topic. All sorts of themes, gritty or otherwise, can be explored and happy endings are not mandatory as they generally are with picture books.

Of course, all my previous tips on researching to find a suitable publisher still apply but the submission rules for longer fiction can be slightly different.

You will still need to write a covering letter but instead of sending the entire text (as in the case of a picture book), as a general guide you will only be required to submit a synopsis of around two or three paragraphs plus a sample of the work; say, two or three chapters. This also has the added advantage that you do not need to have completely finished writing the text before you send out submissions.

Each publisher has different guidelines as to what they expect to receive. Start surfing publisher websites and 'submission guideline' pages before you send anything, and stick to the letter of what they ask for or your work will be summarily rejected. As with my previous advice, do not send out any hand written letters or texts as your submission must be super professional.

It's also worth remembering that many children's publishers produce 'series' fiction for older children from the ages of approximately 5–11 years of age. Look at their websites for details and see if they will accept submissions into those series. If a particular series has a lot of different authors you may be in with a chance.

Very long teenage fiction and longer fiction that crosses over into adult territory may require the services of an agent.

ADULT NON-FICTION

I bet you haven't thought about this? But ask yourself, are you an expert in any particular field? Do you possess knowledge or experience that you could perhaps share with other people? If your answer is yes then you might have a reasonable chance of interesting a non-fiction publisher.

> **NOTE** By non-fiction I am talking about books which are factual as opposed to fictional i.e. from a person's imagination. I've written seven non-fiction books for adults and this is my eighth. Many other children's writers have explored the non-fiction market too.

Your subject matter can be about anything under the sun. Business, money, property, computers, the Internet, animals, fashion, beauty, health, self-help, geography, living abroad, DIY, art and crafts . . . the list is endless. In fact, if you have specialist knowledge, and assuming a lot of other people might find your information useful or fascinating, you might well land yourself a book contract fairly quickly.

Alternatively, are you a teacher with a particular educational interest? It could be a specific subject or just a knowledge and experience in working with children (or adults) with special needs, or with English as a second language. If so, there's nothing to stop you approaching educational publishers and asking what sort of books they might be interested in acquiring.

When approaching a non-fiction publisher you do not need to have written your book, in fact it's better if you haven't. Just follow these guidelines:

- ◆ Research your field to see exactly what books are already out there on the same subject and who publishes them.
- ◆ At the same time, begin to think seriously about your book – the subject matter, the length, who your target audience will be, etc. Try to get some notes down on paper so that you can talk confidently on the telephone.
- ◆ Ring the first publisher on your list and ask to speak to the commissioning editor for non-fiction (or your subject area). Tell them about your idea. If they're interested they'll probably ask you to send

in a proposal. As mentioned above, most publishers provide guidelines for presenting proposals on their websites which they expect you to follow to the letter.

Basically you'll be asked to explain (in writing) why your book will be brilliant, who is going to buy it, how many people might buy it, why a market exists for the particular subject, or angle, what other competing books there are and how well they sell, and how and why your book will be better. They will also expect you to have thought about the cover price, the style and format of the book, etc. All this needs a lot of thought and hard work up front, but hey! This is what authors do.

And before you ask, '*Isn't all this marketing stuff the publisher's job?*', think again. Publishers expect authors to make all the running and they expect to be sold to. If you can't convince them that your book will make millions, who else will?

> **NOTE** Look at the other titles your target publisher produces and consider modelling your proposal on their house style. Make it easy for them to say yes.

A proposal will also normally include a draft contents list. And if you're a first-time author, they will no doubt require a sample chapter or two so they can assess your writing style and competence. Fair enough.

Remember that you'll be more likely to succeed if you either try to fit your book into an existing series or into an area in which your target publisher already specialises. In the same way as you'd be wasting your time to send a picture book to a publisher of romantic fiction, it would be equally pointless to send a proposal for a self-help book to a business publisher.

To conclude: if you have specialist knowledge, good writing skills, and lots and lots of determination (and a willingness to do a great deal of research) the non-fiction market may be a worthwhile one for you to consider if you have trouble selling your children's picture book fiction.

FREELANCE WRITING

Freelance writing is not the same as writing a book. Freelancers produce short articles for newspapers, magazines and commercial (and non-commercial) organisations, usually for a fixed, pre-arranged fee.

Freelancers will not normally get any 'credit' for the work, i.e. their name may not always appear on the article. Sometimes a completely different person will be accredited with the work. That's the nature of the job.

A freelancer will not spend months or years writing a particular piece – they will normally be expected to produce the entire work in a few days or even a few hours! Needless to say, it's very pressurised, and you can have completely manic periods where everyone wants to commission you, followed by long, dry periods in which no work comes in at all.

The Writers' and Artists' Yearbook has a long list of UK newspapers and magazines who accept freelancers' work with details of what sort of thing they want and how to submit work. I also recommend other valuable titles at the end of this book.

There are also lots of Internet sites on which you can bid for freelance writing jobs.

One good way of attracting freelance work is to have published one or more non-fiction titles yourself. I know this is not a very helpful comment but it's true. I've written countless articles on the back of my published non-fiction books on everything from business to health to consumer rights. Maybe a commissioning editor read my book and thought, 'I like her writing style, I wonder whether she'll write a column for XYZ magazine on consumer rights?' This is how the freelance market works.

The other incredibly brilliant thing about non-fiction writing is that so long as the commissioning editor likes your writing style and knows you are reliable and won't miss copy deadlines, you can pick up work on all sorts of topics. With picture book fiction, however, everything depends on the story itself. In some ways you are forever having to reinvent the wheel.

SELF-PUBLISHED PRINTED BOOKS

There are many advantages (and one or two huge disadvantages) of self-publishing your own book. The advantages are:

- ◆ You retain control.
- ◆ You pocket all the profit as opposed to, say, just 5%.
- ◆ You get to choose the illustrator, if you use one.
- ◆ You never get rejected.

As for the disadvantages:

- ◆ You have to meet all the publishing costs.
- ◆ You have to do virtually all the work.
- ◆ You have to sell the books yourself.
- ◆ Unsold stock might end up under the bed!

The topic of self-publishing is a whole book in itself and I cannot possibly cover it in any depth here. But just a little bit of info:

If you plan on self-publishing a picture book or other book that includes illustrations, you need to find and commission an illustrator.

Then you will need a book designer, not to mention a bank loan! Alternatively, do it yourself. To typeset a book you'll need to use a professional publishing program; MS Word is fine for leaflets and booklets but not suitable for a professional-looking 'real' book.

Self-publishing printed books is a very steep learning curve. You'll have to learn all about book binding and paper sizes and layouts. And you'll have to find yourself a professional printer who has experience of the type of book you want. You'll also have to buy a bar code and an ISBN number and include a verso page and copyright notices.

I'd say allow at least six months for the steep learning curve and for re-growing the hair which you've pulled out several times. Finally, once you have 1000 copies of your masterpiece sitting in your hallway, don't forget to send copies to the British Library and other similar organisations in your own country.

At that point comes the rather more tricky job of selling your books into shops and libraries, and online retailers such as Amazon. That's when you'll discover the publishing process was the easy part!

Oh yes . . . and unless you are incredibly lucky, there's no money in it.

The best self-publishing ventures are those which have a very specific purpose or ready-made market. For example, say, a book about ponies written by somebody who has access to all the riding schools in the country.

Another reason people self-publish is to produce something to give away to friends and contacts, for example, a book of poems or an autobiography. In this case all you have to do is produce the books and give them away. No headache trying to sell them!

Many well-known authors have self-published. If Shakespeare and Dickens could do it, why not you? I have self-published a small collection of my children's poems in *Grandma was Eaten by a Shark!* very successfully and I find a ready market for it in the schools I visit.

SELF-PUBLISHED EBOOKS

In the previous section I have discussed the pros and cons of producing your own hard-copy books, but you can dispense with much of the production costs by going down the ebook route instead. In my opinion this is not too difficult assuming you are producing a book containing pure text. But you may still need to pay for professional cover design, if nothing else.

I'm afraid I do not have the space here to explain how to publish an ebook, however there are hundreds of helpful guides on the Internet. To publish your ebook on the Kindle platform (Amazon), simply search for Kindle Direct Publishing. This enormous resource will explain everything you need to know about formatting, pricing, publishing rights, merchandising, tax and much, much more. But it's still going to be a huge learning curve.

If you want to publish an ebook that includes a lot of photographs or illustrations you may need to pay someone to correctly format your book to ensure it's compatible with the major ebook platforms. It's not really a job for an amateur.

If you want to publish a children's picture book story in ebook format, things become even more complicated. This is because picture books use text and illustration **which need to stay fixed together on the page**. Unless you are very conversant with the technology you'll probably need to buy in the expertise to format a fixed-layout book.

Anyway, once your ebook is uploaded to the Internet don't assume it will become an overnight success. Unfortunately you will still have to solve the tricky problem of how to market your book. Amazon currently has 2.5 million ebooks on its 'virtual' shelves, therefore before you go to all the time, trouble and expense of producing the ebook in the first place, ask yourself these vital questions:

- Will this book sell?
- Who will buy it?
- How will potential buyers find out about it?

Big questions – and of course that's one of the attractions of finding a mainstream publisher to buy your text. The financial risk, the production, the technical stuff, the advertising and marketing and product distribution is all taken care of. And you get paid!

But a word of warning. If you cannot find a publisher for your book, and you do not want to self-publish – DO NOT PAY A VANITY PUBLISHER.

VANITY PUBLISHING

A vanity publisher is a shark (posing as a publisher) who advertises for authors, tells you they love your story but then, surprise, surprise, asks for a 'contribution' towards some or all of the costs. Some of these organisations are highly successful simply because there are an awful lot of people out there who are desperate to see their name in print.

They may even be upfront about it and tell you straight away that you'll be footing some or all of the cost but that is not publishing – that's being conned.

If you submit a manuscript to a company who subsequently asks you for money – walk away. Any reputable, genuine publisher who publishes your work will pay you – NOT the other way around.

ONLINE PUBLISHING

Hmm. This book is about getting your children's picture book story accepted by a mainstream, international publisher and turning it into a proper, real-life book. It's not about how to get your work showcased in an online magazine or writing website. And why?

Well, online magazines and writing websites don't normally pay authors anything. And if you've written a great story it would be disappointing to give it away to the entire world for free. Even though you may have to compete with other authors for the 'opportunity' of having your work selected – try to resist. You may even be told (as a friend of mine and would-be author was told recently) that her work was so good it had won an 'award'. But it's still nothing but a con. As are, in my opinion, most online poetry magazines which expect you to pay per submission, or for entry into their latest competition. If you're savvy you can immediately read this as 'money-making venture'.

Another reason to avoid online publishers, including the ones who claim a lot of big-time editors read the stories published on their websites (which again, in my opinion, is rubbish) is that your work is out there literally begging everyone who sees it to copy it or pass it off as their own. And that would be even more disappointing, to have written a great story only to see it appearing in print with somebody else's name on it.

Having said that, there are some excellent and highly reputable magazines, online and hard-copy, in existence that have excellent reputations and a large readership. But although they wouldn't dream of asking you for money, don't expect to be paid anything either.

A FINAL ENCOURAGING NOTE

Whatever you do, keep writing. Produce lots and lots of work. The minute you get a publisher or agent interested in your stuff I can guarantee the first thing they'll say is, 'What else have you got?'. If you're a one-work writer they will not be interested. Above all, do the following:

- Send the manuscript. IT'S NO GOOD TO YOU IN THE FILING CABINET.
- Maximise your chances of having your work accepted by sending your manuscript to suitable publishers.
- Never send original illustrations or your one and only copy of a manuscript.
- Take care over the presentation of your manuscript. Be professional. And keep a note of what you sent where, and when.

- ◆ Do not be discouraged by rejections – all authors get them.
- ◆ Do not write because you think authors make a lot of money. IT'S NOT TRUE. Write because it makes you happy and because you love telling stories.

And once again – SEND THE MANUSCRIPT!

Good luck.

Andrea

Recommended books, websites and writing organisations

This final section of my book lists good writing books, websites and other writing organisations literally bursting with information, help and advice for unpublished (and published) writers as well as details of just a few of the many full and part-time writing courses on offer.

BOOKS

Writers' and Artists' Yearbook
Bloomsbury Publishing PLC
Published annually, this best-selling guide contains ♥Ñpublisher and agent listings (UK and overseas) plus articles on all aspects of the media and how to get published.

Children's Writers' and Artists' Yearbook
Bloomsbury Publishing PLC
As above, only with the main emphasis on children's publishing – another must-have.

Writing for Children
Pamela Cleaver, How To Books

Children's Writer's & Illustrator's Market
Alice Pope, Writer's Digest Books

Writer's Market UK
Robert Lee Brewer, Writer's Digest Books

WEBSITES AND WRITERS' ORGANISATIONS

www.ukchildrensbooks.co.uk
Easy to use and very comprehensive directory of children's publishers as well as links to author and illustrator websites.

www.wordpool.co.uk
Brilliant site for children's writers, parents and teachers includes articles on writing for young children.

www.societyofauthors.org
The professional association for UK authors with a special section for children's writers. Includes many free articles on all aspects of publishing.

http://www.britishscbwi.org/
SCBWI is an enormous writers and illustrators organisation with thousands of members. You don't have to be published to join.

www.thebookseller.co.uk
News and information about the publishing industry.

www.writing-world.com
Hints, tips, links and masses of interesting and informative articles.

www.explorewriting.co.uk
Informative site covering all aspects of writing.

www.behindthename.com
A good place to look if you're stumped for a name for a character.

www.write4kids.com
The Children's Writing Resource Centre is a great US site for children's writers.

www.writersguild.org.uk
Supports writers across media and offers a contract vetting service.

www.fcbg.org.uk
The Federation of Children's Book Groups stages events and a conference every year. Their website includes links to publishers.

www.bookwire.com
Major site for the American book scene, including children's books.

www.shavick.com
Andrea's website.

FULL AND PART-TIME WRITING COURSES

www.arvon.org
The Arvon Foundation runs highly regarded creative writing courses including writing for children.

www.oca-uk.com
The Open College of the Arts is an established distance-learning organisation who offer courses in writing for children

Also, search online to find a host of UK universities offering courses in writing for children.

* * *

Well we are now at the end of my book. I really hope you have enjoyed reading it. And good luck with your publishing career.

Andrea Shavick

Index

How To Write Crime Fiction

Sarah Williams

Available to buy in ebook and paperback

Using examples from contemporary crime writers, this book provides practical pointers, clear explanations and inspiring exercises to develop your skills

It will equip you with a comprehensive overview of all the different kinds of crime fiction to help you identify the sort of novel or short story you're best suited to write. You'll learn about the tricks and techniques used by bestselling authors to make their stories work, with explanations and exercises so that you can hone your own craft and find your own voice – and tell your story in a way that will captivate readers.

From the darkest noir to the most comfortable cosy, from the courtroom to the morgue, crime writers' secrets are laid bare for you to explore, learn from, apply and make your own.

How To Write For Television 7th Edition

William Smethurst

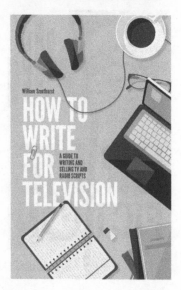

Available to buy in ebook and paperback

'Clear and concise, this book avoids pretentious theorising and provides a practical, no-nonsense guide, invaluable for both new and experienced writers and for potential script editors and producers in drama.' – Diane Culverhouse, literary agent

Soaps, series dramas, plays, situation comedies – television constantly needs new writers. This practical, detailed and inspiring book is full of professional tips and techniques that producers, agents and script editors would give you themselves – if they had the time!

How to Write for Television is packed with excellent guidance and advice, supported by working examples. It includes vital information on how to introduce visual interest as well as invaluable tips on style, structure, plotting and characterisation. It will show you how to successfully *sell* your writing, and includes a comprehensive list of essential contacts for when you're ready to send your screenplay out into the world!

This new and extensively updated seventh edition has everything the aspiring writer for television needs to know.

How to Write Romantic Fiction

Sophie King

Available to buy in ebook and paperback

Learn from leading novelists: this book is bursting with tips from well-known names

Romantic fiction is one of the most competitive areas for a writer to crack. In this book, successful romantic novelist Sophie King (AKA Janey Fraser) will help you:

- Write novels that sizzle – and sell
- Dream up heroes and heroines who breathe (sometimes heavily!) on the page
- Devise contemporary, love-struck dialogue, that's neither slushy nor mushy
- Plan plots that will keep the reader up all night
- Create romantic friction – because love is also about conflict
- Provide fun between the sheets (both the paper and cotton variety)
- Find a happy ending which is both surprising and believable
- Most importantly, get published!

Whether you're a beginner or an already-published writer, you'll find something new in this comprehensive guide to creative writing.